Unpacking Palamism

A Catholic Critique

James Likoudis

Foreword by Fr. Thomas G. Weinandy OFM, Cap.

Essays Selected and Edited by Andrew Likoudis

Published by En Route Books and Media, LLC,
St. Louis, Missouri,
in collaboration with the
Likoudis Legacy Foundation,
Baltimore, Maryland

Make the time

En Route Books and Media, LLC
5705 Rhodes Avenue
St. Louis, MO 63109

Contact us at **contact@enroutebooksandmedia.com**

Cover Design: Andrew Likoudis

©2023 Likoudis Legacy Foundation

ISBN-13: 979-8-88870-118-8
Library of Congress Control Number: 2024930078

All rights reserved. Challoner/Rheims edition published by the Confraternity of Christian Doctrine, 1960. Excerpts from the Catechism of the Catholic Church, second edition, copyright © 2000, Libreria Editrice Vaticana--United States Conference of Catholic Bishops, Washington, D.C. Noted as "CCC" in the text.

theological differences between Catholic and Orthodox, and Likoudis provides his readers with a guide to knowing Mary according to the mind of this 'Pillar of Orthodoxy.'"

— Dr. Jared Goff,
Adjunct Professor of Dogmatic Theology,
Byzantine Catholic Seminary of Ss. Cyril and Methodius;
Co-author, "Palamas Among the Scholastics,"
in *Logos: A Journal of Eastern Christian Studies*

by the *pars maior* of Catholic theologians and can be used with great profit for becoming acquainted with the historically controversial assertions of Palamas and Palamists in both Late Byzantium and by Modern systematic theologians."

— Rev. Christiaan Kappes, PhD, SLD,
Academic Dean,
Byzantine Catholic Seminary of Ss. Cyril and Methodius;
Co-author, "Palamas Among the Scholastics,"
in *Logos: A Journal of Eastern Christian Studies*

"James Likoudis's *Unpacking Palamism: A Catholic Critique* is a most welcome and timely publication. While debate will continue over the compatibility of Palamas's theology and metaphysics with Catholicism, there can be no disputing Likoudis's pivotal role in bringing Palamas into the theological awareness of many Western Christians. Likoudis's trenchant engagement with Palamas over several decades helped set the tone for Orthodox-Catholic apologetics and has had a non-negligible impact in sparking a good deal of more recent scholarly research. This alone more than justifies this publication of Likoudis's collected writings on Palamas. However, it is Likoudis's clear presentation of Palamas's beautiful teaching on the Blessed Virgin Mary, the Mother of all Christians, that sets this book apart. Mary is the key to resolving remaining

"The Churches of the Christian East and West have wrestled for many centuries with the question of the relationship between the uncreated and created realms. Orthodox Archbishop Gregory Palamas of Thessalonica weighed in on this matter in a period of heightened controversy related to the spiritual experiences and contemplative methods of the Athonite Hesychasts (Gk. hesychia "stillness"), forging out of the crucible of both prayer and polemics what he believed to be a theological solution found in the essence-energies distinction in God. The positive reception of this distinction as defined by the Orthodox saint has been by no means univocal in either East or West, and the emergence of a divisive and hyper-polemical neo-Palamite school in modern Eastern Orthodoxy has shed far more heat than light on the subject. In this work, James Likoudis presents a worthy synthesis of his own thinking along with several others on the matter, with varying degrees of sympathy and antipathy towards the Palamite distinction and its possible effect on the prospects of Orthodox-Catholic unity."

— Fr. Daniel Dozier,
Executive Director,
God With Us Eastern Catholic Formation

"Likoudis's concise retelling of the Palamite controversy and problematic readings of Palamism, both among Catholic and Orthodox scholars, as well as his concise summary of Palamas's Mariology, provide an accurate representation of academic positions thereon

"This work represents the capstone of Dr. Likoudis's life-long effort toward reconciling his Eastern Orthodox brethren with the Catholic Church. His concise and informative treatment of Gregory Palamas, the famous and controversial 14th century monk of Mount Athos and Archbishop of Thessalonica, is both highly appreciative and gently critical. On the one hand, Likoudis praises Palamas's ascetical-mystical spirituality and theology of theosis, calling his rich Mariology "sublime" and suggesting that Catholics have much to learn from him. On the other hand, he devotes two chapters to Palamas's controversial notion of God's "uncreated energies," which, though distinct from God's transcendent essence, allegedly do not compromise divine simplicity and yet can be experienced by men as the "Light of Mount Tabor." Likoudis carefully reviews both the writings of Catholics sympathetic with Palamas as well as those who are critical. He devotes two chapters to problematic aspects of Palamism that serve as obstacles to reunion with Rome, noting how some Eastern Orthodox theologians champion Palamas as a rival to St. Thomas Aquinas, yet also noting how others such as Fr. Alexander Schmemann concede the logical necessity of a universal church's need for a universal head in the bishop of Rome. Highly recommended."

— Dr. Philip Blosser,
Professor of Philosophy,
Sacred Heart Major Seminary

Dedication

In loving memory of my cherished wife, Ruth, who walked by my side as my steadfast companion throughout our remarkable 71-year marriage. Together, we built a beautiful life and were blessed to create a flourishing family, welcoming six wonderful children, 35 loving grandchildren, and 44 precious great-grandchildren into the world. As a devout Catholic, Ruth's life was a shining example of piety, humility, and unwavering obedience to God's will. Her faith, hope, and love served as a guiding light for our family, leaving an enduring legacy that will continue to uplift and inspire us. With a heart weighed down by sorrow yet filled with hope, I entrust her soul to the divine mercy of our Lord and the intercession of the Blessed Virgin Mary.

Acknowledgments

I wish to thank:

— My beloved grandson Andrew Likoudis, for his initiative with, and tremendous dedication to, this publishing project, including converting old computer files of some of my writings, converting others from paper to digital, and for all of his work in general in directing the editing and publishing process.
— The Franciscans Friars of the Immaculate for their kindness in allowing me to reprint my presentation delivered at the Sixth International Symposia on Marian Co-Redemption in London, which they sponsored: "The Mariology of Gregory Palamas" (July 2005). This address has been published in volume VI of the superb series *Mary at the Foot of the Cross*, which contains the proceedings of the symposium.
— Emmaus Road Publishing, for their permission to reprint the chapter "Palamism: An Obstacle to the Unity of the Churches?" found with the same title, as Letter Fifty in my *The Divine Primacy of the Bishop of Rome and Modern Eastern Orthodoxy: Letters to a Greek Orthodox on the Unity of the Church* (2023).
— New Advent, for their permission to reprint the entry by Adrian Fortescue on *Hesychasm* as Appendix I.

— The International Theological Commission, for permission to reprint extracts from the document: *Theology, Christology, Anthropology*, Section E., *The Image of God in Man, or the Christian Meaning of the "Deification" of Man*, as Appendix II.
— Herder & Herder, for their permission to reprint Yves Congar's *Note on the Theology of Gregory Palamas*, extracted from his work *I Believe in the Holy Spirit*, as Appendix III.

Table of Contents

Foreword by Fr. Thomas G. Weinandy, OFM Cap. vii

Editor's Preface xiii

1. A Brief Introduction to Palamism 1

2. Palamism: An Obstacle to the Unity of the Churches? 9

3. Further Reflections on Whether Palamism is an Impediment to Reunion 43

4. Fr. Coniaris and the Questionable Theology of Gregory Palamas 61

5. The Mariology of Gregory Palamas 65

Appendix I – *Hesychasm* – Entry by Adrian Fortescue to the original Catholic Encyclopedia 91

Appendix II – Extract from the International Theological Commission document: *Theology, Christology, Anthropology*, Section E., "The Image of God in Man, or the Christian Meaning of the 'Deification' of Man" 103

Appendix III – Yves Congar, *Note on the Theology of Gregory Palamas* 107

Index 127

About the Author 133

Foreword

Gregory Palamas (1296–1359) is an enigmatic theologian. He had the best of intentions in wanting to defend and confirm the Hesychast form of mystical prayer as found on Mount Athos, that is, the continual repetition of the Jesus prayer—"Lord, Jesus Christ, Son of God, have mercy upon me a sinner." By means of this prayer, not only would the practitioner grow in holiness, but he would also attain, ultimately, a mystical experience like that experienced by the apostles at the Transfiguration on Mount Tabor. This transfiguring light was judged to be the uncreated energies that radiated from the divine essence of God himself.

This understanding came under attack, for it seemed to undermine God's singular oneness. By making a real distinction between who God is in himself (his divine essence), and the way he expresses himself outside of himself (his uncreated energies), God is no longer simply the one God. A justification for such a distinction, and thus a validation of the Hesychast mystical experience, was Gregory's goal when he undertook to further expound and clarify the distinction between God's essence and his divine energies. However, Palamas's efforts to conceive and articulate such a defense and clarification led him to hold what many—both past and present—believe is a heretical view of God and of his relationship to the created order.

Gregory Palamas's underlying and overriding error in conceiving and articulating his essence and energy distinction can be found in his employing a Neo-Platonic understanding of God's transcendence. God does not exist in a singular distinct manner from all else that is, rather he exists in a manner that places an infinite gulf between himself and all else that is. This breach must be maintained to protect God's divine transcendent nature, yet a way must be found for him to nonetheless be active in the finite realm so as to provide a relationship to it, such as through mystical experiences. Gregory was convinced that such a solution is found in that God's essence, who he is in himself, remains immutably perfect in its transcendent nature, yet he can bridge this infinite gulf between himself and the finite realm and humankind through his eternal divine energies that emanate out from him in a Neo-Platonic manner.

The philosophical and theological problem that ensued, is that humankind is never related to God as he is in himself, but only through some lesser expression of himself, that is, through his divine energies. Palamas was aware of this concern and attempted in many and various ways to overcome it. However, in the end, he admitted that he found no satisfactory solution, while still maintaining that such a distinction between God's essence and his energies must be upheld at all costs.

Blinded by his Neo-Platonic presuppositions, Gregory never fully grasped that his proposal was not in accord with biblical revelation. What we find within the Old Testament is God himself acting in time and history without jeopardizing his divine transcendence. This understanding finds its ultimate expression within the Incarnation. The Son of God comes to exist as man, without ceasing to be truly God in so becoming. What Palamas failed to realize is that God is not transcendent in himself—that is, at some infinite distance from the created order. Transcendence pertains not to God in himself, but in his relationship to all else. In himself, God is simply God, but in relationship to all else he is transcendent, in that he exists in a distinct manner from all else. Palamas is completely ignorant of the great Judeo-Christian, and so biblical, mystery—that the transcendent God can act salvifically in time and history without endangering his distinct divine manner of existing. Although much more could be said by way of critique of Palamas's position, the above introduces James Likoudis's book, *Unpacking Palamism: A Catholic Critique*.[1]

Likoudis, in his opening chapter, provides a brief, but excellent, critical account of Gregory's theological thought. In the light of Palamas's thinking, Likoudis next asks whether his teaching is an obstacle to the unity of the churches.

In accord with what was briefly noted above, Likoudis offers, in chapter two, an extensive history of the theological debates and controversies surrounding Gregory's thought. After a lengthy treatment of various Eastern and Western critiques of Palamas's distinction between God's essence and his energies, it becomes evident that his theology is an obstacle to unity among the churches. Such is the case not only between the Greek and Latin churches, but also within the Eastern Orthodox Churches themselves.

---

[1] For a fuller exposition and critique of Gregory Palamas's teaching see my "Gregory Palamas, Essence and Energy: Eradicating Falsehood and Establishing Truth," in *International Journal of Systematic Theology*, published online in April 2023, and will be included in a future printed issue.

In chapter three, Likoudis addresses further issues that are impediments to ecclesial reunion. Once again, after examining various accounts of Palamas's thought, both positive and negative, Likoudis concludes that, because of his erroneous views, his philosophical and theological doctrines cannot be the source and foundation for unity.

To support his own negative assessment of Gregory, Likoudis next examines Fr. Coniaris's denunciation of Palamas's questionable theology. Having read these four chapters, one can only conclude that Likoudis's critique of Gregory of Palamas is devastating. Gregory may have been a holy man, but he was an inept philosopher and an incompetent theologian.

However, there is a saving grace in chapter 5 where Likoudis treats Palamas's Mariology. Gregory had a great love for and deep devotion to Mary, particularly under the title of Mother of God. Here, unlike within his essence and energy distinction, Palamas is both spiritually inspiring and theologically helpful. Although it is not fully developed, Gregory promotes and supports the doctrine that Mary was immaculately conceived. Moreover, he positively addresses Mary as the mediatrix of all graces—though such a notion is itself a controversial issue both within the Catholic and Orthodox Churches.

Likoudis's book concludes with three helpful appendices taken from various sources.

As the editor, Andrew Likoudis has performed a valuable service to the theological academy and to the ecclesial communities of the East and the West by making available his grandfather's exposition and critique of Gregory Palamas's major writings. For his dedicated work, the reader can be grateful.

— Thomas G. Weinandy, OFM, Cap.,
Capuchin College, Washington DC

Editor's Preface

In the course of one's lifetime, certain tasks present themselves as duties of love rather than mere obligations. Editing this manuscript of my grandfather, (honoris causa) Dr. James Likoudis's work on the complex and often misunderstood topic of Palamism and its implications for the Eastern Orthodox Church is one such endeavor for me.

Dr. Likoudis's work delves into the theological intricacies of Gregory Palamas and his teachings, referred to as Palamism. His teachings have been, as my grandfather painstakingly outlines, a source of considerable theological strife, affecting not only the unity within the Eastern Orthodox Church but also its relationship with the Catholic Church. Through a careful examination of both ancient and contemporary theological writings, Dr. Likoudis attempts to untangle the complicated web of Palamism. Within this book he explores topics such as the unity of the Churches, the notion of the distinct essence and energies of God, the procession of the Holy Spirit, and the beatific vision.

While editing this manuscript, I have endeavored to preserve the integrity of my grandfather's work. The richness of his thoughts is interlaced with a meticulous attention to detail, and I've sought to capture that same rigor in the editorial process. To this end, any modifications to the text have been kept to a minimum, aiming only to enhance clarity and readability.

It is a privilege to serve as the editor of this volume. May this book not only pay homage to the depth and breadth of my grandfather's scholarship, but also serve as a catalyst for further study and discussion in the years to come.

— Andrew Likoudis
Feast of St. Therese of Lisieux,
October 1, 2023

I.

A Brief Introduction to Palamism

Gregory Palamas (1296–1359) was a monk from the famous monastery at Mount Athos in Greece, and later a cleric who dissented in key ways as the Archbishop of Thessalonica. He was the most important Byzantine Greek spiritual writer and theologian of the fourteenth century. His distinctive teachings eventually received the approval of three Byzantine synods in 1341, 1347, 1351, and, frankly, they were imposed by brutal force. One of the most respected representatives of Byzantine monasticism, Palamas became the head of a monastic party whose neo-Hesychastic spirituality would have a profound effect on the Byzantine Greek and Slav monastic world for centuries. The Palamite theological synthesis appears, however, to have been ignored by many theologians in subsequent centuries, and opposition to it is clearly seen in the Russian Church's removing Palamite elements in its 1769 revision of the *Synodikon*,[1] a revision which also included expunging anathemas that condemned Palamas's chief opponents. However, because of the emergence of a neo-Palamite school of theology in the last century, which seeks to legitimize Palamas's doctrine of divine essence and uncreated energies as normative for all Eastern

---

[1] An official declaration of the Orthodox faith.

Orthodoxy, there have been renewed debates concerning the fidelity of Palamite doctrine to the teaching of the Greek Fathers and the classical Hesychastic spiritual tradition.

Hesychasm comes from the Greek *hesychia,* which means "holy stillness" or "quietness." It refers to the monastic life as found among the ancient Greek, Coptic, and Syrian Fathers from the third century forward. They were spiritual masters of prayer—oral, mental, and contemplative—and their ascetical and saintly lives stimulated the growth of monasticism in the Byzantine world.

Defending the practice of Hesychastic Prayer and attempting to safeguard the patristic doctrine of divinization, Gregory Palamas had taught that there was a real distinction between the essence of God and his energies. These energies proceed from the essence of God and are uncreated. The term deity may rightly be applied to these energies. According to Palamas, man cannot participate in the unknowable essence of God; he can only participate in his energies which can, moreover, be experienced in the form of light. This is the same *uncreated light* which was manifested to the apostles at the Transfiguration of Christ, Palamas argued, and can be seen by the saints during this life. Palamas's teaching, upon which his entire mystical theology is based, was attacked as contrary to the simplicity of God's essence by both "*Latinophrones,*" "Latin-minded sympathizers" like the brothers Kydones, using the arguments of Western Scholasticism, and the more rigid anti-Latin polemicists and humanists such as Barlaam the Calabrian, Gregory Akindynos, and Nikephoros Gregoras. The Byzantine church was convulsed by the violent theological quarrels waged over Palamism, which resulted in persecution, confinement, and exile of the leading anti-Palamites. Palamas's major doctrines were upheld by the local councils held at Constantinople in 1341, 1347, 1351, and 1368. According to the late Kallistos Ware and some other Eastern Orthodox theologians, the Palamite distinction between essence and energies is "not merely a private speculation or an 'optional extra,' but an indispensable part of the faith"—a "dogma."[2]

In an important article, "*The Philosophical Structures of Palamism*," Dr. Rowan D. Williams has treated the philosophical weaknesses of Palamas's teaching concerning the essence and energies of God, observing further: "Many scholars, by no means unsympathetic to the Western tradition, *have serious doubts upon whether the Palamite distinction of essence from energy is really a legitimate development*" of earlier patristic teaching.[3] Similarly, in his remarkable doctoral dissertation on the Hesychastic Controversy in the fourteenth century, Professor Lowell Clucas believes

---

[2] Kallistos Ware, "God Hidden and revealed: The Apophatic Way and the Essence-Energies Distinction," *Eastern Churches Review* 7, no. 2 (1975): 125–136. See also his reply to critics, "The Debate about Palamism," *Eastern Churches Review* 9, nos. 1–2 (1977): 45–63. He took issue with Dr. Rowan Williams's view of the irreconcilability of Palamism and Thomism. In Ware's opinion, the Hesychastic Controversy should not be construed as a conflict between "unionists" and "anti-unionists," nor should Palamism be interpreted as an anti-Thomistic response.

[3] Rowan D. Williams, in *Eastern Churches Review* 9 (1977): 27–44.

that "the insistence of Aquinas that the distinction between essentia and operatio in God *was only a mental distinction* is more in accord with the best Byzantine patristic thought than Palamas." He traces the root deficiencies of Palamas's theological system to the epistemological errors of an extreme neo-Platonism, which succumbed to the temptation of transforming an emanationist noetic cosmos into pseudo-divine energies: "No such extreme Platonism had ever been introduced into Orthodoxy before."

Professor Clucas explains that:

> In looking around for the necessary theological conceptions to employ in defense of the "facts" of this "experience" of the knowable "energies" manifested by the unknowable "essence" of God, Palamas seized in fact upon the Platonic ideas as they were adopted by Christian Neoplatonism. But in doing so, he converted them from their ontologically somewhat confused status as constituents of the "noetic" creation yet "contemplated essentially around God," and subsumed them under the Light of Tabor which the monks claimed to be the central "fact" of their "experience," and which, since they most certainly did believe it was seen, makes its impact upon the Hesychasts as a visible light and indeed almost as a physical force.[4]

Professor Clucas finds—as did the fourteenth-century Byzantine

---

[4] Lowell Clucas, *The Hesychast Controversy in Byzantium in the Fourteenth* Century, vol. 2, 549; cf. chapter ten *in extenso*.

Chapter 1: A Brief Introduction to Palamism

Thomistic opponents of Palamism—that the latter must be regarded as,

> a seriously flawed theology, at least by the conceptual standards of the analytical theology of the great theologians involved in the formation of orthodox theology up through the Iconoclast Controversy, that is, from Athanasius to St. John of Damascus. For among those of them who became involved in making definitions, postulates, and defining relationships between man and God, one can usually find the rejection of the idea that God's energy is perceivable, except in certain special senses quite different from Palamas. They reject the application of the essence-energy distinction as a conception to be applied to God, since, they often claim, it can only be an analogy drawn from the created world, which our intellects apply to God in order to understand that which is beyond all earthly comparisons. And they reject a middle ground of being between the created and the uncreated. They do not, of course, reject the conception of theosis[.] [D]ivinization, and indeed the divinization of man through Christ is often a major aspect of their thinking and teaching. But they do not, like Palamas, define God's energy as perceivable, that is, they do not formally connect divinization to an immediate perception by corporeal vision of divine light. They always stop short of defining it this way, and they implicitly or explicitly deny the theological

distinction to which Palamas resorted in order to rationalize the undoubtedly real experience of theosis.[5]

It may be added here that Professor Clucas's dissertation on the Hesychastic Controversy brings some valuable correctives to the influential writings of Fr. John Meyendorff on Palamas and Palamism.

For varied assessments of Palamite doctrines by contemporary Catholic theologians, readers may find interesting the "*Note on the Theology of Gregory Palamas*" originally found in Fr. Yves Congar, OP's erudite work on the Holy Spirit.[6] [It has been added to this work for convenience, serving as Appendix III.]

The Jesuit theologian, Fr. Bertrand de Margerie, SJ, has also considered the views of some Catholic theologians who attempt a more benign view of Palamas's teachings, but he expresses his doubts as to the possibility of harmonizing the five fundamental Palamite theses, as "canonized" by the fourteenth-century Constantinopolitan synods, with the Catholic Faith.[7]

In addition, the Franciscan theologian Fr. Peter Damian Fehlner, OFM Conv., has observed the following concerning the Palamite denial of the beatific vision:

---

[5] Clucas, *A Consideration of The Hesychast Controversy*, vol. 1, 130–131.

[6] Yves Congar, OP, *Je Crois en L 'Esprit Saint* (Paris: Les Editions du Cerf, 1980), vol. 3, 94–106; An English edition is also available under the title *I Believe in the Holy Spirit* (New York: Herder & Herder, 2016).

[7] Bertrand De Margerie, SJ, *Les Perfections du Dieu de Jesus Christ* (Paris: Les Editions du Cerf, 1981), 137.

Chapter 1: A Brief Introduction to Palamism

Palamism (the monastic spirituality of the fourteenth-century Archbishop of Thessalonika, Gregory Palamas) was not and is not overtly and intentionally anti-hierarchical; indeed it has always enjoyed a certain amount of support from members of the Byzantine hierarchy as well as the approval of a number of medieval Byzantine synods. Its stress on the absolute primacy of Christ and what would seem to be an equivalent support for the doctrine of the Immaculate Conception, as well as its adamant opposition to rationalism in theology—have made it seem to many, not a few Catholics included, an attractive form of orthodox spiritual renewal. There remains, however, one serious flaw in the Palamite position, a doctrinal one, which again calls into doubt the other dogmatic points concerning which Eastern Orthodoxy unfortunately finds itself at odds with Catholic Tradition.

Whereas the Catholic Church has always taught both the possibility and fact of the beatific vision as having the divine essence as its object—particularly throughout the fourteenth century, the same century which also saw the rise of Palamism among the monks of Mount Athos—Palamism in seeking to defend the divine transcendence by guarding against an arid rationalism, has always denied that very doctrine *by placing a sharp division between the divine essence on the one hand* (considered beyond intelligibility for the created mind) *and the divine energies* (by which creation comes to be and in which the created mind can experience the bliss of heaven). It is not too difficult to perceive in such a position the rest of an anti-dogmatic, anti-metaphysical bias, pointing ultimately to a purely "experiential" and therefore "pantheistic" religion.

Because from a Catholic point of view the primary duty of the hierarchy is to teach us about the nature of God, viz., the mystery of three Persons in one essence, the radical denial of the possibility of such understanding in any form necessarily implies an anti-hierarchical bias manifested towards that supreme hierarch in particular, namely the Successor of St. Peter, who has proclaimed and defended the real possibility of the beatific vision to fallen man. There is, therefore, not only a logical nexus between the rejection of the *Filioque* and the repudiation of papal primacy in the Church, but there is also one between the repudiation of papal authority and the Palamite denial of the possibility of the beatific vision (and therefore the intelligibility of the divine essence).[8]

---

[8] Fr. Peter Damian Fehlner, OFM Conv., "Healing an Ancient Schism: Theological Reflections," *Social Justice Review*, September–October 1985, 150. In a private correspondence dated February 27, 2014, Fr. Peter Fehlner revised his previous views on the essence/energies distinction and the Filioque controversy. Influenced by Rev. Christiaan Kappes' scholarly work, Fehlner's reassessment aligns with a Scotistic interpretation, advocating a kind of "formal distinction" between essence and energies, similar to the understanding presented by George Scholarios, and consistent with Catholic orthodoxy.

2.

Palamism:
An Obstacle to the Unity of the Churches?

Scholars continue to debate whether aspects of Palamas's teachings represent an authentic development of the thought of the ancient Greek Fathers and Doctors, or whether, as Palamas's fourteenth-century critics have charged, he indeed deviated in his doctrine, and thereby ignited a controversy which shook the Byzantine Greek Church.

The controversy over his teachings continues today, especially since a neo-Palamite school of theology began to emerge in the 1930s among Greeks and Russians. These scholars have included George Florovsky, Vladimir Lossky, Fr. Jean Meyendorff, Archimandrite Cyprian Kern, Archbishop Basil Krivoscheine, John Romanides, Fr. Dumitru Stanisloae, Metropolitan Hierotheos Vlachos, George Varrois, George Mantzaridis, and Christos Yannaras, among others. They all regard Palamas's major teachings as "dogma" and have utilized them either to distance themselves from the Catholic Church, or to denounce the Church because Catholic theologians—past and present—have generally regarded the Palamite teaching on God's essence and "uncreated divine energies" unfavorably—and even as heretical. Some neo-Palamites, such as Christos Yannaras and Fr. Michael Azkoul, have even gone to the extreme of claiming that the definitive separation between Eastern and Western Christianity should be seen in the Catholic rejection of Palamas's teaching, which, again, placed a real distinction between the essence of God and His alleged uncreated energies. They have charged that all the Catholic "heresies," especially the *Filioque*, as well as the secular humanism and nihilism of the West, flow from that rejection. To the contrary, Palamas's novel teachings increased doctrinal tensions already existing between Rome and the separated Eastern churches.

In his Angelus address on August 11, 1996, Pope St. John Paul II commented on the:

> development of Eastern theology, which, even, in the centuries that followed the age of the Fathers and the sad division with the Apostolic See, led to profound and stimulating perspectives at which the whole Church looks with interest. Although there is still disagreement on this point or that, we must not forget that what unites us is greater than what divides us.[1]

The Pope noted that Eastern spirituality has "amassed a very rich experience" from the earliest days of the Church,[2] with the works of writers from both the classical Hesychastic period—fourth to

---

[1] Pope St. John Paul II, Angelus address, August 11, 1996, no. 1; as given in *L'Osservatore Romano*, weekly English edition, August 21, 1996.

[2] John Paul II, Angelus address, August 11, 1996, no. 2.

ninth centuries—and the later neo-Hesychastic period being collected in the famous collection entitled *Philokalia*, which Nicodemus the Hagiorite compiled at the end of the eighteenth century. St. John Paul II also stated:

> The Hesychast controversy [of the fourteenth century] marked another distinctive moment in Eastern theology. In the East, Hesychasm means a method of prayer characterized by a deep tranquility of spirit, which is engaged in constant contemplation of God by invoking the name of Jesus. There was no lack of tension with the Catholic viewpoint on certain aspects of this practice. However, we should acknowledge the good intentions which guided the defense of this spiritual method, that is, to emphasize that man is given to unite himself with the Triune God in the intimacy of his heart, in that deep union of grace which Eastern theology likes to describe with the particularly powerful term of "theosis," "divinization."...
>
> How many things we have in common! It is time for Catholics and Orthodox to make an extra effort to understand each other better and to recognize with the renewed wonder of brotherhood what the Spirit is accomplishing towards a new Christian springtime.[3]

In the thirteenth and fourteenth centuries, a neo-Hesychastic

---

[3] John Paul II, Angelus address August 11, 1996, no. 2.

movement began that claimed to be in doctrinal continuity with the primitive Hesychasm of earlier centuries. Many of the monks on Mount Athos, long regarded as the "guardians of Orthodoxy" against the Latins, were to favor key Palamite doctrines considered necessary for Christian perfection.

Key elements of the Palamite philosophical-theological synthesis aroused fierce controversy between Palamas and fellow Byzantines in his day. His leading opponents included Barlaam of Seminara, Gregory Akindynos, Isaac Argyros, John Kyparissiotes, Demetrios and Prochoros Kydones, Theodore Dexios and Nicephoros Gregoras. Interestingly, some of these opponents were unionists who desired the reunion of the Catholic and Orthodox Churches, while others fiercely opposed both "the Latin heretics" and the Palamites. Though they had differences among themselves, the anti-Palamites decried Palamas's exaggerated mysticism and strange philosophical terminology. They criticized:

1. Palamas's distinguishing the unknowable essence of God from his knowable and participable "uncreated divine energies." For Palamas, God's essence—i.e., his divine nature—is completely mysterious, transcendent, unknowable, and unapproachable. Human beings, however, can be divinized through God's uncreated energies, which they teach are distinct from His essence. Both here and in the next world, men can share in God through His uncreated energies bestowed by deifying (or divinizing) grace.

2. Palamas's teaching that one can see in this life the uncreated energy of God in the vision of the "Light of Tabor," in other words, such light as made manifest at Christ's Transfiguration, which is an uncreated radiance that is, at times, visible to human eyes transformed by the divine energies. Thus, this uncreated divine light can be perceived with one's bodily eyes. In Palamas's words, "that Light is the light of divinity and is uncreated."[4]

3. His claim that God's essence is completely unapproachable, even by the saints in heaven.

It would appear for Palamas, and both his medieval and modern followers, that the divinization of the Christian necessarily implies the Palamite dogma that there is a real distinction in God between His essence and His purported uncreated energies. There can be no question that the doctrine of theosis or divinization, i.e., the soul's becoming God-like, is both of biblical (2 Pet 1:4), and patristic origin[5] and can also be found in classical Hesychasm. However, Palamism went beyond classical Hesychasm. Palamas claimed that those seeking union with God can see the Uncreated Light, but problematically described that Light as the very "uncreated energies" of God, which are supposedly nothing but God Himself; and yet, he adds, these uncreated energies are also somehow distinct from God's divine nature. The spiritual experiences

---

[4] Gregory Palamas, Hom. 34.
[5] CCC 460.

of neo-Hesychast monks, influenced by the reported visions of light by the charismatic monk Symeon the New Theologian (949–1022), were reportedly also experienced by Gregory Palamas, and they led him to develop a theological system which defended a mystical experience involving the physical consciousness of grace. *The Oxford Dictionary of the Christian Church* explains neo-Hesychasm in this manner:

> The immediate aim of the Hesychasts was to secure what they termed "the union of the mind with the heart," so that their prayer became "prayer of the heart." This prayer of the heart leads eventually, to those who are especially chosen by God, to the vision of the Divine Light, which, it was believed, can be seen—even in this present life—with the material eyes of the body, although it is first necessary for a man's physical faculties to be refined by God's graces and so rendered spiritual. The Hesychasts held this light to be identical with the Light that surrounded the Lord at His Transfiguration on Mount Tabor, and to be none other than the uncreated energies of the Godhead. They considered this Light, and not (as in Western theology) God's essence,[6] to be the object of the beatific vision.[7]

---

[6] See CCC 1028; 1045.

[7] Elizabeth A. Livingstone, Frank Leslie Cross, eds., *The Oxford Dictionary of the Christian Church* (Oxford: Oxford University Press, 2005), 768.

Souls purified by ascetical exercises—including certain psychosomatic breathing exercises, though Palamas claimed these were not central but merely helpful for beginners—can thereby see the same divine light that the apostles saw on Mount Tabor at Christ's Transfiguration. The mystical phenomenon of saints who become transfigured by a supernatural light was similarly explained as light identified with nothing less than the uncreated energies of God, and which manifest the same divine glory that shone from Jesus at His Transfiguration.

Catholic doctrine has not accepted a real distinction, if indeed it be a real distinction in God that was made by Gregory Palamas, between the "unknowable essence" of God and His "uncreated energies." The neo-Palamites declare these uncreated energies are many, infinite, and knowable. But no ecumenical council has ever predicated any plurality in God other than that of the Trinity. Such a real distinction in God would undermine the simplicity of God. As the Dominican theologian Fr. Aidan Nichols, has stated,

> God is not *sunthetos*, made up of parts, as are creatures. How can there be an aspect of God not included in the divine essence? Are not *essentia* and *operatio* distinct in God only 'formally'?[8]

Similarly, Fr. Bernard Schultze, SJ, noted, "The Catholic theologian cannot accept an exaggerated negativism nor a distinction in

---

[8] Fr. Aidan Nichols, OP, *Light from the East* (London: Bloomsbury Publishing, 1999), 54.

God which tends to deny the absolute simplicity of the completely perfect Spirit." He has also pointed out that if the essence of God were absolutely unknowable to the human intellect, as Palamas held, then one would not only be *unable* to know that it is unknowable, but one would *also* be incapable to know if there were a distinction to be posited between God's essence and His energies, because God's essence/nature would, again, be unknowable. In other words, how can you make a distinction between two realities when you've already posited that one of those realities, i.e., God's essence, is itself *absolutely* unknowable by human persons?

In Palamas's system, there is God's essence and Persons *and* energies and, contrary to Catholic teaching, it is the "uncreated energies" which come into contact with man in the process of divinization (or sanctification), not the very Persons of the Holy Trinity, who remain inaccessible as belonging to the unapproachable divine essence. The Palamite claim that God's "uncreated light" can be seen in this life by one's bodily eyes would involve some type of "beatific vision" in the present life, or it confuses a created radiance produced by God with the uncreated God Himself. Furthermore, a number of astute authors have commented on the philosophical incoherence of Palamism in its considering the divine essence as beyond the Divine Persons, just as the Divine Persons are beyond the uncreated energies. In effect, this would result in Palamism's "removing the Trinity from our salvation."[9] This judgment is confirmed by the Lutheran theologian Reinhard

---

[9] See Dorothea Wendebourg, *Geist oder Energie?* (Munich: Chr. Kaiser Verlag, 1980).

Flogaus, who, in a remarkable article, has shown how Palamas was at odds with the standard Catholic doctrine as represented by St. Augustine:

> Augustine identifies God's giving of Himself with the person of the Spirit, while Palamas perceives it as divine energy. It is evident to Gregory [Palamas] that at Pentecost only the energy of the Holy Spirit was poured out on the disciples, while his hypostasis [Divine Person[10]] stayed invariably imparticipable even then. At the back of this reasoning lies Palamas's understanding of participation as necessarily introducing a division in that which is participated. This compels him to admit only the possibility of [man's] participation in the divisible divine energy, whereas participation in the person of the Spirit must be disavowed.[11]

The Palamite claim that God's "uncreated light" can be seen by bodily eyes in this world as an experience of deification—i.e., divinization, or "sanctification" in Western terms—would mean that the glory of God can be seen with the eyes of our flesh in this life. But the teaching of Scripture is that the direct vision of God in *the full glory of His divinity* is beyond the sight of any mortal creature

---

[10] CCC 468.

[11] See Reinhard Flogaus, "Palamas and Barlaam Revisited: A Reassessment of East and West in the Hesychast Controversy of Fourteenth-Century Byzantium," *St. Vladimir's Theological Quarterly* 42 (1998): 1–32.

in this world. For the Transcendent God dwells in "inaccessible light" (1 Tim 6:16), and the Beloved Disciple has written that "no man has at any time seen God" (John 1:18), meaning, in His unmediated divine essence, which would exclude encounters that the disciples had with the Incarnate Word during His earthly ministry. The Lord God had told Moses, "I will be gracious, and will show mercy on whom I shall show mercy, but you cannot see my face; for man shall not see me and live" (Exod 33:19–20). In the supernatural order of grace revealed by Christ, the immediate face-to-face vision of God has been reserved to the beatific vision in heaven where, as St. John revealed, "We shall be like him, because we shall see him as he really is" (1 John 3:2). St. Paul similarly writes of the beatific vision awaiting the just in heaven when he says, "We see now through a mirror in an obscure manner, but then face to face. Now I know in part, but then I shall know even as I have been known" (1 Cor 13:12) It is Catholic doctrine that only in heaven will the one and Trine God become the immediate object of our sight, and this with the supernatural aid of the "light of glory." The beatific vision of God was always enjoyed in this life by Christ in his human nature, but the exceptional visions of Christ and other mystical experiences, in which the saints may indeed have been granted a certain awareness of the presence of the Trinity (cf. 2 Cor 12:1ff.), are not to be confounded with the beatific vision which, as an experience, is final. In the beatific vision, Catholic doctrine further notes that the blessed souls experience the divine essence directly but without comprehending the Infinite God's essence completely. As theologians have written, the blessed see God *totum sed non totaliter* ("whole but not wholly"), and according to the degree and intensity of grace they possessed as earthly wayfarers. Thus, Catholic doctrine indeed holds that God is unknowable in that He cannot be known with a *comprehensive* vision by any created intellect. However, in the supernatural order of grace, man can be elevated to know God immediately and intuitively in heaven, and see Him face-to-face in the beatific vision with the help of the light of glory. As the Council of Florence (1439) defined, "The souls of the saints know by clear intuition the one and Triune God as He is in Himself, yet one more perfectly than another according to the diversity of their merits."[12]

By this definition the Church condemned the Palamite error, utilized by Mark of Ephesus during the Council debates on the *Filioque*, which would deny the beatific vision by maintaining that the divine nature, as it is in itself, cannot be even supernaturally seen by the created intellect. Contrary to the Palamite error, the well-known *Confession of Dositheos* (1672) unequivocally states, "After their death [the saints] behold clearly the Holy Trinity."[13] Also, in Peter Mohila's *Orthodox Confession of Faith* (1640), we read that,

> this joy and gladness [of heaven] will be no other than the beatific vision of the Holy Trinity. Every desire of wisdom and all goodness will cease in this vision; for by gazing attentively upon God, we will see all things in Him and we

---

[12] Council of Florence, *Laetentur Caeli*, sixth session.
[13] *Confession of Dositheos*, Decree VIII.

will experience all joy.[14]

It is significant that, from the seventeenth century into the early twentieth century, not a few Russian and Greek theological manuals distanced themselves from Palamite doctrines.[15]

But what then was the Light of Tabor that was seen by the apostles in the Transfiguration of Christ, the splendor of which Palamas identified as "the uncreated energy of God"?

In one of his earlier works, Cardinal Charles Journet replied to the Palamite contention of Vladimir Lossky, who argued that the Transfiguration proved we can see the glory of God with the eyes of our flesh in this world, and that no change occurred in Christ at the Transfiguration, but only in the consciousness of the apostles, "who received for a brief time the faculty to see their Master as He really was, shining with the eternal light of His divinity." The Swiss Catholic theologian noted:

> First of all, its source and its cause were the uncreated light and glory of the divinity of the [Incarnate] Word.
>
> For, as St. John explains, the glory which the Word possessed from eternity in the bosom of the Father remained His, even when He became flesh. The glory of Tabor, then, was the illumination of the holy humanity of Christ by this glory; it was the created effect of this glory as

---

[14] Peter Mohila, *Orthodox Confession of Faith*, q. 126; as given at http://apostles-creed.org.

[15] See, e.g., *Dictionnaire de Theologie Catholique*, "s.v. Palamite (*Controverse*), 1811–1816."

it was received in the weak and passible [i.e., capable of suffering] body of Christ. "The divinity," as St. John Damascene says, "was so invincibly impassible in spite of the passible humanity, that it could make the body participate in its brilliance and glory." And before him St. Andrew of Crete had already written, "Since the apostles could not endure the miraculous presence in Christ's immaculate body of the brilliance which shone forth from the divinity of the Word to which that body was hypostatically united, they fell prostrate on the ground." It is by reason of this hypostatic union that the humanity of Christ is always and everywhere adorable, whether plunged in the suffering of the crucifixion or in the glory of the Transfiguration. Finally, the light of the Transfiguration consisted in an impression of the divine glory on the external world, on the garments of Christ and on the luminous cloud which enveloped the apostles. Gregory of Palamas, then, had good reasons for wishing to adore the light of Tabor, but no less valid were the reasons that led [his opponent] Barlaam to consider it as a corporeal and transitory phenomenon. If these two had only expressed their convictions more exactly, truth would have triumphed instead of confusion and dispute. . . .[16]

But if it were true that at the moment of the Transfiguration the

---

[16] Cardinal Charles Journet, *The Wisdom of Faith* (Westminster, MD: Newman Press, 1952), 26–27, 198–199.

body of Christ was not really changed, if it were true that it did not pass from a passible state to a glorious state, if it were true that Christ's body was constantly transfigured and glorious, then we would have to conclude that the passible state of Christ the suffering and death of Christ, were illusions, since they consisted only in appearances. Thereby we would rejoin the very ancient error of Docetism [which denied Christ's "true humanity"[17]].

Moreover, such an opinion on the Transfiguration was certainly not the unanimous teaching of the Oriental Church. Speaking of that mystery, for instance, St. Cyril of Alexandria remarks that Christ was then "transfigured by an excellent and divine splendor."[18] Basil of Seleucia is of no other opinion: "While the disciples considered what had taken place, suddenly Christ was transformed before them. His appearance changed, and clothed in a tunic of light, He afforded them a brilliant sight."[19]

Another indictment has been made by neo-Palamite authors that deserves a response, namely, their charge that Catholic rejection of the Palamite distinction between divine essence and energies has resulted in the loss of the patristic doctrine of "deification" in the Catholic Church. They charge that "clinging to its theology of the 'divine simplicity,' there is no place for deification . . . in Roman Catholicism," an argument that has been made and repeated by such neo-Palamites as Christos Yannaras, Fr. Michael

---

[17] CCC 465.

[18] St. Cyril of Alexandria, "Homily on the Transfiguration," *PG*, LXXVII, col. 1011.

[19] Basil of Seleucia, "Sermon on the Transfiguration of the Lord," no. 2, *PG*, LXXXV, col. 457

Azkoul, and Metropolitan Hierotheos Vlachos.

No, the Catholic Church has not set aside the patristic doctrine of "deification" or "divinization" so strongly stressed by the Greek Fathers of the Church. Many modern Catholic writers, including Pope St. John Paul II, have emphasized how Christians are made by baptism "sharers of the divine nature" (2 Pet 1:4), thus entering into "communion with the Most Holy Trinity."[20] In Pope St. John Paul II's apostolic letter *Orientale Lumen*, he pays due tribute to the rich monastic spirituality of the Eastern tradition that remains alive in both the Eastern Catholic and separated Greco-Slav churches. He also acknowledges the theology of the Eastern Fathers concerning the *comprehensive* unknowability of God, writing as follows:

> [The goal of the Eastern Christian] is participation in the divine nature through communion with the mystery of the Holy Trinity. . . .
>
> Participation in Trinitarian life takes place through the liturgy and in a special way through the Eucharist, the mystery of communion with the glorified body of Christ, the seed of immortality. In divinization, and particularly in the sacraments, Eastern theology attributes a very special role to the Holy Spirit: through the power of the Spirit who

---

[20] See Appendix II for an extract from the International Theological Commission, on the topic of divinization or theosis, as the Catholic Church understands it.

dwells in man, deification already begins on earth; the creation is transfigured, and God's Kingdom inaugurated.

The teaching of the Cappadocian Fathers on divinization passed into the tradition of all the Eastern churches and is part of their common heritage. This can be summarized in the thought already expressed by St. Irenaeus at the end of the second century: God passed into man so that man might pass over to God. This theology of divinization remains one of the achievements particularly dear to Eastern Christian thought.

On this path of divinization, those who have been "most Christ-like" by grace and by commitment to the way of goodness go before us: the martyrs and the saints. And the Virgin Mary occupies an altogether special place among them. . . .

Although strongly emphasizing Trinitarian realism and its unfolding in sacramental life, the East associates faith in the unity of the divine nature with the fact that the divine essence is unknowable. The Eastern Fathers always assert that it is impossible to know what God is; one can only know *that* He is, since He revealed Himself in the history of salvation as Father, Son, and Holy Spirit.[21]

The doctrine of "theosis" or divinization by grace (Latin theology would refer to "sanctifying grace") begins in baptism. In receiving

---

[21] John Paul II, Apostolic Letter *Orientale Lumen* (May 2, 1995), no. 6; emphasis mine.

baptism, a person is justified, in other words, forgiven of "original sin and all personal sins, as well as all punishment for sin."[22] Baptism also makes one an "adopted son of God" through the indwelling of the Blessed Trinity in his justified soul.[23] This doctrine of "theosis" remains the common patrimony of both Catholics and Eastern Orthodox, though certain false mystics have distorted it, falling into certain errors such as pantheism. Divinization does not mean, of course, that one literally becomes God, but only God-like, as that great mystic St. Gregory of Nyssa explained: "To become like God means to become just, holy, and good, and such like things."[24] In addition, "The goal of the life of virtue is to become like God."[25] Such expressions as "theosis" or *theopoesis* do not signify that the Christian becomes God, which is existentially impossible, but rather denotes, as the French Catholic theologian Louis Bouyer says, "the certainty of the genuine reality of our supernatural adoption, involving, as the Epistle of Peter says, our participation in the divine nature."[26] In this participation, wherein we are changed by grace, we do not lose our identity as individual human persons, and thus we are not absorbed by the divine nature

---

[22] CCC 1263.

[23] CCC 1265.

[24] Gregorius [St. Gregory of Nyssa], *The Lord's Prayer* [and] *The Beatitudes*, trans. Hilda C. Graef (Westminster, MD: Newman Press, 1954), 42.

[25] *St. Gregory of Nyssa: Homilies on the Beatitudes*, eds. Albert Viciano, Hubertus Drobner (Boston: Brill, 2015), 254.

[26] Fr. Louis Bouyer, *Dictionary of Theology* (New York: Desclee Company, 1965), 115.

of God. Fr. Matthias Joseph Scheeben, the greatest Catholic speculative theologian of the nineteenth century, and one who was also greatly influenced by the Greek Fathers, summarizes the transformative process: "Our nature is not changed into another nature by grace, so that we lose what we already possess. [Habitual or sanctifying] grace communicates a new quality to the soul, by which it is transformed into the supernatural image of God."[27] In addition, in his magnum opus *The Mysteries of Christianity*, Fr. Scheeben explained at length the divinization of Christians, affirming that the concept has its equivalent in the doctrine of "sanctification" developed by Western theologians. He also takes care to observe:

> Ordinarily we refer to the deification and rebirth of man during this life as sanctification rather than transfiguration. We do not call it transfiguration because here the divine fire poured forth upon us gives only a hint of its brightness in a few faint rays, displaying for the most part the warmth of its love. A further reason is that, for the present, the divine splendor of God's children lies dormant in them as in a bud or seed, to burst forth into full magnificence only on the other side of the grave. But the luster of this faint glow, the loveliness of this bud, is an earnest of the immensity of that glory which God will shower upon

---

[27] See Fr. Matthias Scheeben, *The Glories of Divine Grace* (Gastonia, NC: TAN Books, 2002).

us in the future life."[28]

All of the above indicates that, on one hand, there are elements of neo-Hesychastic spirituality—e.g., understanding the stages of purification, illumination, and deification; and the nature of contemplation—which are identical with those lived by the great Catholic mystics of the West. On the other hand, there are certain points of doctrine where the neo-Palamites deviate from Catholic teaching:

First, Catholic doctrine does not accept an ontological or real distinction in the nature of God. Some scholars believe that Palamas has read into the ancient Fathers his own confused concepts and categories. That is, in attempting to distinguish the essence of God from His purported "uncreated energies," Palamas erroneously combined Aristotelian and Platonic philosophical notions. Consequently, for example, Palamas tried to distinguish between God's "supraessence—or "super-essential essence—from his "essence." But there is no "supraessence" or "essence" over and above the Trinity of Persons. No ecumenical council of the Church has ever taught any plurality in God other than the Trinity. The question as to whether Palamas intended a real or merely conceptual distinction in God is crucial. Most authors think he intended a real distinction between God's essence and energies, as his language appears to imply a real distinction. However, this would fatally compromise God's divine simplicity. It was not unusual for medieval thinkers to reify concepts, positing in reality a distinction that

---

[28] Fr. Matthias Scheeben, *The Mysteries of Christianity*, trans. Fr. Cyril Vollert, SJ (St. Louis: B. Herder, 1946), 654–655.

only existed in the mind of the theologian. Palamas may have been groping for the right words, i.e., through the language of conceptual distinction, but, in any case, he did not find them to assure the safeguarding of the divine simplicity in God.

Thus, Palamas appears to have developed a novel theology in order to defend the doctrine of divinization (or deification) and the spiritual life as lived in the neo-Hesychastic tradition. However, in attempting to posit a real distinction between the unknowable essence or inner being of God, and his knowable and participable energies or acts of power, Palamas has caused much confusion through the philosophical-theological language he chose to express himself.

Second, it would be contrary to Catholic teaching to state that it is the "uncreated energies" of God which come into contact with man in the process of divinization (sanctification) and *not* the very Persons of God, as if the Father, Son, and Holy Spirit remain utterly inaccessible to man because they belong to the wholly unknowable and imparticipable divine essence.

Third, it is true we can never fully comprehend God, either in this life or in the next. Indeed, as mere creatures, we can never know the Infinite God as He knows Himself. Palamas, however, appears to deny that the divine essence, as it is in itself, will be supernaturally seen by the created intellect in the beatific vision. Neo-Palamite Fr. Michael Azkoul is adamant:

> Not even uncreated grace permits the creature, angelic or human, to behold the unspeakable and unapproachable essence of God." This denial contradicts the truth, defined by

Pope Benedict XII, that the blessed souls in the beatific vision will "see the divine essence with an intuitive vision and even face to face.[29]

Fourth, as to a number of neo-Palamites' denying the existence of "created grace," blaming St. Augustine for this "heresy," and teaching that divinization or "participation in the divine nature is possible only if grace is uncreated,"[30] they appear ignorant that Palamas himself had a concept of "created grace." As the aforementioned Reinhard Flogaus has written,

> Augustine of Hippo accepted the same basic definition of grace as participation in the divine nature as did the Greek Fathers. The differentiation between created and un-created grace is found in Augustine and Palamas. A significant difference, however, can be seen in the fact that Augustine identifies God's giving of Himself with the Person of the Spirit while Palamas perceives it as divine energy, since the hypostasis stayed invariably imparticipable even then. Although Palamas and Augustine disagree about the character of uncreated grace, they are still in agreement about its distinction from created grace or gift.[31]

---

[29] Pope Benedict XII, apostolic constitution *Benedictus Deus* (1336), as given at ewtn.com.

[30] Fr. Azkoul, *Once Delivered to the Saints*, 97.

[31] Flogaus, "Palamas and Barlaam Revisited," *St. Vladimir's Theological Quarterly*, 14–15.

In his refusal to admit that the Holy Spirit Himself indwells the souls of the just, Palamas is found once again at odds with the patristic tradition. Moreover, a number of neo-Palamites have been quite mistaken in accusing St. Thomas Aquinas of ignoring the patristic doctrine of divinization. The Angelic Doctor had no qualms in using the word "divinization" and agreeing with St. Athanasius that "we are made gods by grace"—an expression that he took special pains to explain carefully to avoid any pantheism. As mentioned previously, Aquinas even listed divinization as one of the reasons why God became man. He noted that one reason for the Incarnation is "the full sharing of divinity, which is the true happiness and purpose of human life." Aquinas quotes approvingly St. Augustine's "Sermon 128": "God was made man than man might become God."[32] In the *Catechism of the Catholic Church*, Aquinas himself is quoted as declaring, "The only-begotten Son of God, wanting to make us sharers in his divinity, assumed our nature, so that He, made man, might make men gods."[33] In his writings, the Angelic Doctor has further observed that it is through the created gift of sanctifying grace that we are made God's friends and that the Divine Persons themselves are given to us so that we can enjoy their presence. The Catholic theologian Fr. Piet Fransen, SJ, has refuted certain misunderstandings concerning the Church's teaching on created and uncreated grace, noting that *the uncreated Spirit of God is given in created grace*. Indeed, it is, in fact, the indwelling of the Blessed Trinity, which is

---

[32] *PL* 39, 12997.
[33] St. Thomas Aquinas, *Opusc.* 57:1-4, quoted in CCC 460.

the living ground and source of that created grace, that makes us just and holy:

> In [Catholic] theology, uncreated grace stands for God Himself insofar as He communicates Himself to man in love. In contradistinction to this, created grace signifies the result God's Self-communication produces on man. Evidently that result cannot be God Himself; therefore, it is something other than God, something created, a gift from God. Created grace may not be conceived apart from the divine indwelling. Created grace is not something standing in between God and us. It does not act as a screen between God and us since it comes into being only because of and within the gesture by which God unites us immediately to Himself. Created grace is at once the fruit and the bond of the indwelling, originating in the indwelling and sustained by the indwelling; it raises us into an ever-deepening actualization of the indwelling on earth and in heaven. It is of no great consequence to know how many kinds of grace there are, and what they should be called or how they could be defined and described. *The main point is that grace enables us to have personal contact with God.* Created grace has no other *raison d'etre*.[34]

It should be noted that the Catholic theology of uncreated and created grace actually helps explain divinization as a sharing in God's

---

[34] Fr. Peter Fransen, *Divine Grace and Man* (New York: New American Library/ Mentor- Omega Books, 1965) 122–143, emphases added.

own nature and not simply His energies.

Fifth, it cannot be ignored that Palamas outright denied that the Holy Spirit proceeds from the Father and the Son in one eternal spiration of love. He said "the pride of the presumptuous Pope" caused the addition of the *Filioque*. More to the point, he declared this Catholic doctrine "heretical," arguing that it implies two distinct origins of the Holy Spirit. This accusation had been repudiated by the Second Council of Lyons (1274) as a "*calumnia*." The *Filioque* in no way challenges the "monarchy of the Father." Nevertheless, Palamas told the Latins in his polemical writings, "Never will we receive you in communion as long as you say that the Holy Spirit proceeds also from the Son." Here again, as Orthodox theologians have recalled, it was Palamas's struggle to provide an adequate theology of the procession to buttress resistance to the Latins—who were "heretical" and "under anathema"—as well to the "Latin-minded" unionists which also stimulated him to develop his distinction between essence and energy in God.

Sixth, in his writings, of course, Palamas also rejected traditional Catholic doctrine on the Pope's universal authority in the Church. Palamas accused the Latins of "failure to return from heresy . . . although [their Roman throne] was the greatest and the leader of the patriarchal thrones of outstanding eminence." Unfortunately, the judgment of the Old Calendarist Archbishop Chrysostomos of Etna appears well-founded, namely, that,

> the very structure of Palamite theology disallows *any* attribution of universal jurisdiction or authority, except in the traditional sense of 'honor' or 'eminence,' to *anyone* in

the Church.[35]

For Palamas and his neo-Palamite followers, orthodox teaching and Church authority are not only identified with but determined by the saints of neo-Hesychastic,

> spiritual enlightenment, which, in turn, is the product of a true and genuine encounter with God shared by all enlightened individuals and equally. Hesychasm is a direct condemnation of Papism.[36]

In Palamite theology, consequently, those "spirit-filled" and "deified" saints, i.e., who live the neo-Hesychast life well, are the ones who best represent the "consciousness of the Church" in resolving questions of doctrine, even more than the Pope, or patriarchs, or assemblies of bishops, because these ecclesiastical leaders may lack experiential knowledge of the spiritual dimensions of the Christian religion. The result of this perspective is the fatal devaluation of the Church's visible hierarchical authority, in which Palamas opts instead for those allegedly illumined and enlightened by the Holy Spirit. In this excessively spiritualized (and "mystical") ecclesiology of Byzantine neo-Hesychasts, Christ's own establishment

---

[35] Archbishop Chrysostomos of Etna, "St. Gregory Palamas and the Pope of Rome,"
Orthodox Tradition 13, no. 2: 26–27, emphases added.

[36] Archbishop Chrysostomos, "St. Gregory Palamas and the Pope of Rome," 27.

of the Petrine ministry in the Church to head the universal episcopate has suffered eclipse, replaced by a magisterial subjectivism that claims to be guided by the Spirit. (See further my book *Ending the Byzantine Greek Schism*, chapter three, in which I note how the denial of the procession of the Holy Spirit from the Father and the Son results in the denial of Christ's establishing a supreme visible authority in His Church.)

As with other medieval Byzantines, however, the Catholic view of the primacy of Peter in the gospels was too traditional and strong for Palamas to be totally forgotten. Thus, in his "Homily 28" on the Feast of SS. Peter and Paul, Palamas speaks in a way that would surely surprise some modern Orthodox detractors of Peter's primacy among the apostles:

> The first traitor, who incited the first man to desert God, saw Him who had earlier made Adam, the father of the human race, later recreating Peter as the father of all true worshippers. He not only saw, but also heard the Creator saying to Peter: "Thou art Peter, and upon this rock I will build my church" (Matt 16:18). Once the prince of evil found this out, being the epitome of wicked envy, he tempted Peter, the first leader of God's faithful people, as he had previously tempted Adam, the founder of the race of men. . . .
>
> What does the Lord do? Since Peter has shown that he has not lost his love for Him and has now acquired humility as well, He openly fulfills the promise made long before and tells him, "Feed my lambs" (John 21:15). When He was

referring to the company of believers as a building, He promised to make Peter the foundation stone, saying, "Thou art Peter, and upon this rock I will build my church" (Matt 16:18). On the other hand, when He was talking in terms of fishing, He made him a fisher of men with the words, "From henceforth thou shalt catch men" (Luke 5:10). But when He speaks of His disciples as sheep, He sets Peter over them as a shepherd, saying, "Feed my lambs, feed my sheep" (John 21:15-17)....

Thrice Christ appoints him over His sheep and lambs, placing under him the three categories of those being saved: slaves, hirelings, and sons, or, alternatively, virgins, chaste widows, and those honourably married....

Once Peter had made this heartfelt confession, the Lord ordained him Shepherd and Chief Pastor of His whole Church....

When Peter resorted to repentance, he not only recovered from his fall and obtained forgiveness, but was also appointed to protect Christ's Church.[37]

Such above texts have been coupled by medieval and modern Eastern Orthodox with a denial that the Bishop of Rome as Peter's successor has any more authority by divine right than any other bishop. They have alleged that every bishop is a Peter in his own

---

[37] Palamas, Hom. 28, nos. 5, 7, 8, 9, 13; as cited at www.omhksea.org/archives/2445. See also *The Homilies of Saint Gregory Palamas*, vol. 2, trans. Christopher Veniamin (Waymart, PA: St. Tikhon's Seminary Press, 2004).

local Church, and no bishop has a supreme authority over the entire assemblage of local churches that make up the universal Church. This ecclesiology collapses, however, under its own weight as being totally non-historical, because the unique privileges and prerogatives of the See of Peter in Rome were acknowledged by the Fathers and councils of the first millennium. To attempt to make every bishop the Successor of Peter in his indefectible primacy of faith, would result in attempting to make each bishop indefectible in faith, which is an obvious absurdity, because opposing bishops could both claim the divine protection of infallibility, and yet at least one of them would be wrong on the doctrine(s) at issue. There is certainly a legitimate sense in which each bishop expresses the Faith of Peter in the Church, but this only if his authority is exercised in collegial unity with the Roman Pontiff, who is the chief pastor of the Church, "the perpetual and visible source and foundation of the unity both of the bishops and of the whole company of the faithful."[38]

Neo-Palamite authors have insisted that the errors of Palamas constitute the teaching of the entire Eastern Orthodox communion. Fortunately, this does not seem to be the case, because no ecumenical council—the magisterial standard still considered by many Orthodox as indispensable for dogmatic resolution—has ever approved as dogma the various Palamite theses, despite their having been widely held by many of their theologians. Thus, it is difficult to accept what is known as "Palamism," as official Orthodox dogma, binding on all the autocephalous Orthodox churches.

---

[38] Second Vatican Council, *Lumen Gentium*, no. 23.

Chapter 2: Palamism: An Obstacle to the Unity of the Churches?

Because neo-Palamites elevate Palamas's theological opinions into dogma, and regard his particular neo-Hesychastic spirituality as *alone* "Orthodox," there exists a serious barrier to reunion with the Catholic Church. With respect to the core Palamite doctrine on the essence and energies of God, it also appears that such writers as Fr. Meyendorff, Lossky, Yannaras, and Bishop Kallistos Ware do not agree on the exact meaning Palamas placed in God regarding the distinction. Moreover, it is significant that the younger Greek theologians today appear to be distancing themselves from the Palamite theological synthesis, which has enjoyed a monopoly in Greece as much for political, as theological motives.

In view of the above factors, it would appear that if Palamas's teaching is demonstrated as not jeopardizing the divine simplicity in God, and if his other teachings were acknowledged by Orthodox prelates as *"theologoumena,"* in other words, theological opinions open to debate, rather than dogma requiring assent, his philosophical-theological synthesis would not serve as an insuperable obstacle to the prospect of doctrinal reunion with the See of Peter.

Many issues have been raised over the years to pronounce the Catholic Church "heretical," and so as departing from Tradition and the teaching of the first seven ecumenical councils. However, if an ecumenical council is considered the criterion for orthodox belief regarding all the issues contested by Eastern Orthodox theologians, then one must ask:

1. What ecumenical council ever declared the doctrine of the *Filioque* heretical?

2. What ecumenical council ever declared heretical the Catholic doctrine of papal primacy of universal jurisdiction, i.e., stemming from Peter's primacy over and among the apostles?
3. What ecumenical council ever declared the Catholic doctrine of the Intermediate State (termed Purgatory) heretical?
4. What ecumenical council ever declared the use of azymes (unleavened) bread for the Eucharist heretical?
5. What ecumenical council ever declared the Catholic doctrine of the Immaculate Conception heretical?
6. What ecumenical council ever declared Catholic baptism and other sacraments invalid, as some Orthodox leaders, in fact, hold?
7. What ecumenical council ever declared that there is a real distinction between essence and "uncreated energies" in God?
8. What ecumenical council ever declared that the event of the Transfiguration did not happen just once in history, but that others in this earthly life have similarly attained the vision of God as Uncreated Light?
9. What ecumenical council ever declared that "created grace" does not exist?
10. What ecumenical council ever declared that the Pope as chief pastor of the Church cannot define dogma, but that only an ecumenical council can?
11. What ecumenical council ever defined that the dogmatic decrees of an ecumenical council need no confirmation

from the Successor of Peter as chief pastor of the entire Church?

What provides promise for a future resolution of the doctrinal disputes between Eastern Orthodoxy and the Catholic Church? I would argue this: that practically every Catholic doctrine ardently opposed by certain Orthodox polemicists has *also* been shared by *other* Orthodox leaders, past and present. The doctrinal incoherence and contradictions found in modern Eastern Orthodoxy is, quite frankly, due to the centuries of political and cultural estrangement, then disobedience, and then open schism from the Roman Pontiff as visible head of the Church Militant, this same Pontiff who, as chief pastor of God's people on earth, presides over the entire Church to preserve its visible unity and catholicity.

I conclude this chapter, in observing how the Russian Orthodox theologian Fr. Alexander Schmemann refuted the basic objection posed by more "mystical" theologians, who think that Christ's establishing a visible head for a visible Church is in contradiction to His being the invisible head of His universal Church:

> The important point is . . . for us to see that in the light of this doctrine [of a universal Church] the need for and the reality of a universal head, i.e., the bishop of Rome, can no longer be termed an exaggeration. If the Church is a universal organism, she must have as head a universal bishop as the focus of her unity and the organ of supreme power. The idea, popular in Orthodox apologetics, that the

Church can have no visible head, because Christ is her invisible head, is *theological nonsense*. If applied consistently, it should also eliminate the necessity for the visible head of each local church, i.e., the bishop. *Yet it is the basic assumption of a "catholic" ecclesiology that the visible structure of the Church manifests and communicates its invisible nature.* The invisible Christ is made present through the visible unity of the bishop and the people: the head and the body. To oppose the visible structure to the invisible Christ leads inescapably to the Protestant divorce between a visible and human Church which is contingent, relative, and changing, and an invisible Church in heaven. We must simply admit that if the categories of organism and organizational unity are to be applied primarily to the Church universal as the sum of all its component parts (i.e., local churches), then the one, supreme, and universal power as well as its bearer becomes a self-evident necessity, because this unique visible organism must have a unique visible head. Thus, the efforts of Roman Catholic theologians to justify Roman primacy not by mere historical contingencies but by divine institution appear as logical. Within a universal ecclesiology, primacy is of necessity power and, by the same necessity, a divinely instituted power; we have all this in a consistent form in the Roman Catholic doctrine of the Church.³⁹

Fr. Schmemann's candid statement is truly remarkable. He goes on to reject the doctrine of the Church as a "universal organism" in favor of a "Eucharistic ecclesiology" as developed by Fr. Nicholas Afanassieff. But the doctrine of a universal Church was as deeply imbedded in the consciousness of the Fathers of the ancient Church as was the ancient teaching that it is the "Eucharist which makes the Church." It is also good to note here, as Cardinal Henri de Lubac has observed, that,

> "Christ in his Eucharist is truly the heart of the Church," and that the Church is "neither Latin nor Greek, but universal." In the universal Church, the See of Peter presides over the episcopate and serves as its "one and only visible center."⁴⁰

---

³⁹ Fr. Alexander Schmemann, "The Idea of Primacy in Orthodox Ecclesiology," in Fr. Meyendorff, ed., *The Primacy of Peter*, 151, emphases added.

⁴⁰ See Cardinal Henri de Lubac, SJ, *The Splendour of the Church* (Glen Rock, NJ: Paulist Press/Deus Books, 1956), 92, 162–165.

3.

Further Reflections on Whether Palamism is an Impediment to Reunion

Many Catholic authors have acknowledged the genuine spiritual and theological riches found in the writings of the 14th century Byzantine monk and Archbishop of Thessalonica, Gregory Palamas. Despite some aspects of Palamas's theology remaining problematic, his mystical spirituality and teachings have been favored by some Western and Eastern Catholics[1] both here, and abroad, who, surprisingly, venerate Palamas as a Saint (especially following the confusing 1974 decision of the Congregation for Eastern Churches allowing Byzantine Catholics to celebrate the *"Feast of St. Gregory Palamas"*). Some writers took advantage of a November 30, 1979, homily in Ephesus by Pope St. John Paul II which referred to *"St. Gregory Palamas."* They appear unaware that in the official *Acta Apostolicae Sedes* of the Holy See, this was corrected

---

[1] See: Maloney, George, SJ, A Theology of Uncreated Energies. Milwaukee, WI: Marquette University Press, 1976; Raya, Archbishop Joseph. The Face of God. (Mckees Rocks, PA: God With Us Publications, 1984; Zimany, Roland D. "The Divine Energies in Orthodox Theology", (Diakonia. Vol. 11, no. 3 (1973) 281-285.); Rev. David Hester, S.S. "St. Gregory Palamas-Defender of Orthodoxy". Diakonia, vol. 15, no. 2 (1980), 174-184.

to "*the Orthodox bishop Gregory Palamas.*" They also appear unaware that questionable teachings of Palamas have been heartily utilized by Eastern Orthodox writers to refute the "heresies" of the Catholic Church and to resist ecumenical efforts to restore full communion between the Orthodox Churches and the See of Rome. Gregory Palamas was one of the leading Byzantine ecclesiastics who opposed Unity with Rome. This essay will summarize serious objections to what has been deemed the major doctrinal teachings of what has been termed "*Palamism.*"

It is interesting that contemporary scholarly debate continues about whether aspects of Palamas's teachings (intended to safeguard the reality of *deification/divinization/theosis*—that is, the genuine communion of God with the soul) represent an authentic development of the ancient Greek Fathers and Saints or whether he indeed innovated in matters of doctrine. This was charged by his 14th century Byzantine contemporaries.[2] The resultant controversy shook the Byzantine Greek Church with theological consequences to this day. Interestingly, both 14th century Byzantine Greek unionists seeking the restoration of Unity with Rome and intransigent anti-unionists challenged Palamas's philosophical and theological teachings as "novelties" and "heresies." Palamas was especially charged with falsifying the teaching of the Fathers on "essence" and "energy" which are, in fact, identical in God. In placing a real distinction between the essence and energies of God,

---

[2] E.g., Barlaam of Calabria, Gregory Akindynos, Nicephoros Gregoras, Theodore Dexios, Isaac Argyros, Demetrios and Prochoros Cydones, etc.

he was accused of endangering the Church's doctrine on God's Absolute Simplicity. *Contra* Palamas, the operations and energies of God are held to be the created effects of the divine essence.

After some centuries' eclipse of Palamism among Orthodox theologians, the 1900's saw a revival of Palamite hesychastic spirituality prepared for by the publication of the *Philokalia*, a collection of 14th century and earlier, mystical writings. As mentioned previously, the 1930's saw an emergence of the neo-Palamite school of theology among Greeks, Russians, and Romanians who sharply reacted to the critical examination and evaluation of the writings of Gregory Palamas made by the erudite Catholic scholar Martin Jugie, AA in the *Dictionnaire de Theologie Catholique*.

Palamas's present followers adhere to the definitions of the Byzantine Councils of 1347 and 1351 held in Constantinople which endorsed the theology of Palamas. The Council of 1351 was imposed on the Byzantine Church by imperial force and the persecution of opponents. It issued a Tome in defense of Palamism which can be summarized as follows:

1. There is in God a distinction (*diadkrisis*) between the essence and the energies or energy (It is equally legitimate to refer to the latter either in the singular or in the plural);
2. The energy of God is not created but uncreated (*akistos*);
3. This distinction between the uncreated essence and the uncreated energies does not in any way impair the divine simplicity [of God]; there is no 'compositeness' (*synthesis*) in God;
4. The term 'deity' (*theotis*) may be applied not only to the

essence of God, but to the energies;
5. The essence enjoys a certain priority or superiority in relation to the energies, but not in His essence;
6. Man can participate in God's energies but not in His essence;
7. The Divine energies may be experienced by men in the form of light—a light which, though beheld through men's bodily eyes, is in itself nonmaterial, 'intelligible' (*noeron*) and uncreated. This is the uncreated light that was manifested to the Apostles at the Transfiguration on Mount Tabor, that is seen during prayer by the saints in our own time, and will shine upon, and from, the righteous, at their resurrection on the Last Day. It thus possesses an eschatological character: it is 'the light of the Age to Come.'
8. No energy is to be associated with one divine person to the exclusion of the other two, but the energies are shared in common by all three persons of the Trinity.

Palamas thus stressed that the transcendent God remains eternally hidden in His Essence, but communicates with man through His "uncreated divine energies." Thus, man cannot participate in God's imparticipable Essence, but can be divinized by partaking in His "uncreated divine energies." God, in His Divine Simplicity is at the same time both personally imparticipable and personally participable to us. In defense of this Palamite teaching on the nature of God which was attacked by 14th century Byzantine Greek humanists (as well as by some Catholic Dominican Thomists of the period) as a heretical novelty, neo-Palamite theologians have

Chapter 3: On Whether Palamism is an Impediment to Reunion

proceeded to contend that all the Catholic "heresies" (especially the 'Filioque' and the Petrine supremacy of the Pope) as well as the secular humanism and nihilism of the West, flow from the rejection of Palamas's "dogma" concerning the nature of God. For the majority of Orthodox theologians in Europe and North America, the heart of the doctrine of Gregory Palamas is "the real distinction in God of the essence and the uncreated energies." Dr. Jeffrey D. Finch has written that *"the Defense of the Palamite essence-energies distinction [has been] a touchstone of Orthodox identity in the West for most of the remainder of the twentieth century, even until the present time."*[3] Moreover, to such Orthodox hierarchs as the Greek Orthodox Metropolitan of Nafpaktos, Ierotheos Vlachos, *"the basic distinction between the Orthodox Church and Papism is found in the doctrine concerning the uncreated nature and uncreated energy of God."* This doctrine (paraded as the key to all the alleged doctrinal deviations of Catholicism), appears to have even replaced the centuries-old 'Filioque' dispute as the most serious obstacle in the way of the Reunion of the Catholic and Orthodox Churches. The classic theological teaching of St. Augustine and St. Thomas Aquinas, the pillars of traditional Western and Catholic theism, and who affirmed Catholic teachings opposed to Palamas's major theses, resulted in much fierce Neo-Palamite polemi-

---

[3] Finch, Jeffrey D. "Neo-Palamism, Divinizing Grace, and the Breach Between East and West" in Christensen and Wittings' Partakers of the Divine Nature: The History and Development of Deification in the Christian Tradition (2007).

cal invective against them. Palamas (canonized by a synod in Constantinople in 1368) became exalted as the East's "universal Doctor" and the *Anti-Augustine/Aquinas* who vindicated the apophatic and mystical theology of the East against the godless Rationalism, Legalism, and arid Scholasticism of the West.

Acting as the authentic spokesman for the monastic hesychasm of the 14th century, Palamas sought therefore to justify theologically, with his essence-energies distinction, the avowed goals of those practicing the ascetic and spiritual life familiar to the monks of Mt. Athos. Oftentimes, after the long repetition of the famous "Jesus Prayer" ("Lord Jesus, have mercy on me a sinner"), and striving for unitive deification [*theosis*] of union with Christ, this "prayer of the heart" is given a reaffirming vision of God's Uncreated Light or Energy. This Light, as previously noted, was declared identical with the "Taboric Light" seen by the Apostles at His Transfiguration and was one of the eternal energies. As Palamas stated in his *Triads*,

> He who participates in the divine energy . . . becomes himself, in a sense, light; he is united with the light and with the light he sees in full consciousness all that remains hidden for those who have not this grace; for the pure of heart sees God [the light].

Palamas's claim that God's "Uncreated Light" can be seen bodily eyes in the world as an experience of *theosis* would mean that the glory of God can be seen with the eyes of our flesh in this life. But this was denied by all those who held the traditional teaching of the Church that the direct vision of God in the full glory of His divinity is beyond the sight of any mortal creature in this world. For the Transcendent God dwells in *"inaccessible light"* (1 Tim. 6:16) and the Beloved Disciple wrote: *"No man at any time has seen God"* (Jn. 1:18). Certainly, for Catholics, in the supernatural order of grace revealed by God, the immediate face-to-face vision of God has been reserved to the Beatific Vision in heaven where, as St. John disclosed: *"We shall be like Him because we shall see Him as He really is."* (1 Jn. 3: 2). Traditional Eastern and Western teaching held that the Saints see God directly but not completely or comprehensively. Not even with the supernatural aid of the *"light of glory,"* was there a *comprehensive* vision of the Tri-personal essence of God, for it is beyond the complete grasp of any created intellect.[4] The opponents of Palamas, moreover, vigorously denied that Tradition had any place for his theory of *energies*.

Interestingly, past Orthodox Confessions of Faith departed from Palamism when they taught:

> And not only are the Saints while on their pilgrimage regarded as mediators and intercessors for us with God, but especially after their death, when all reflective vision being done away, they behold clearly the Holy Trinity in Whose infinite light they know what concerns us.[5]

---

[4] For a refutation of the Palamite view of the Light of Tabor, see Charles Journet's *The Wisdom of Faith*, (*Newman Press*, Westminster, Maryland (1952) 26-27; 198-199.

[5] *Confession of Dositheos*, 1672.

> The joy and gladness of Heaven will be no other than the beatific vision of the Holy Trinity. . . . Every desire of wisdom and all goodness will cease in this vision; for by gazing attentively upon God we will see all things in Him and we will experience all joy.[6]

In Palamas's doctrine, the essence of God is forever unknowable; in heaven we will not see the essence of God, we will not see "face-to-face" the Blessed Trinity in the glory of heaven. What the beatified human being sees in Heaven is not the divine essence of God but rather its uncreated energies. Writing in 1969, A. Karpozilos of Yale University explained that,

> the doctrine of the divine energies ineffably distinct from the divine essence, is the dogmatic basis of the real character of Eastern Orthodoxy and its doctrine of grace. The [Palamite] distinction in no way divides God's nature in two parts—knowable and unknowable—but signifies two different modes of the divine existence in the essence and outside of the essence.[7]

It is the "uncreated energies" of God which come into contact with man in the process of divinization (sanctification) and not the very Persons of God who remain inaccessible as belonging to the divine absolutely unknowable and imparticipable essence. In his *Logoi*

---

[6] *Orthodox Confession of Faith* of Peter Mohila, 1640.
[7] Karpozilos, Apostolo D., *St. Thomas and the Byzantine East* (1969)

apikeitikoi, Palamas specifically wrote: "*The Person of the All-Holy Spirit is not from the Son, nor is he given by the Son, nor does anyone receive him, but rather the divine grace and energy.*"[8] Palamas's opponents held to the traditional teaching that what St. Peter meant by our being "*partakers of the divine nature*" (2 Pet. 1: 4) is being indwelt by the Persons of the Holy Trinity, NOT "participating in the divine energies". The Scriptures and Fathers speak of the Divine Persons dwelling in the just. There is no notion of "uncreated divine energies" dwelling in us but rather the Divine Persons themselves. Palamas's tampering with traditional doctrine is further reflected in his teaching that on Pentecost it was not the person of the Holy Spirit which descended on the Apostles and other disciples but rather the "uncreated energies of the Holy Spirit." For the neo-Palamites, these "uncreated energies" are declared many, infinite, eternal, and knowable. But no Ecumenical Council has in its Trinitarian definitions ever predicated any plurality in God other than that of the Trinity. Only God, Father, Son and Holy Spirit is uncreated. In his extreme apophaticism, Palamas posited God as a Supra-Essence who is absolutely unknowable and is above and beyond the Trinity, treating the Persons of the Trinity as distinct from the substance of God, and thereby departing from the patristic tradition. The best scholars on Palamism seem to agree that it was a *real ontological* distinction between God's essence and His attributes which Palamas made. This conclusion flows from the neo-Palamites' assertion of an infinite multiplicity

---

[8] Gregory Palamas, *Logoi apikeitikoi*, ii, 48.

of divine energies which are not to be identified with His Super-essential Essence (a Supra-Essence above or beyond the Trinity). In making this real distinction (one that is not merely mental, notional, or conceptual) between the unknowable essence and knowable "uncreated energies" of God, Palamas was seen by his critics (both in the 14th century and now) to endanger the Absolute Divine Simplicity of God by bringing composition into the Godhead, into His very Being. As Demetrios Kydones who introduced the thought of St. Thomas Aquinas into Byzantium by his translations of St. Thomas' *Summae,* noted:

> What reasonable person could bear with those who say that the essence of the one God is one thing and [the attributes of] His goodness, power, life, wisdom and all that the Holy Scripture and the common arguments of all people ascribe especially to God, are another thing? . . . In this way we shall think that God does not have the utmost simplicity, but that he is a multiplex being and a mixture; that he contains within Himself so many things and so different from each other?

Interestingly, C.S. Lewis once wrote that he considered Palamas's teaching on the Essence of God and His Energies "strange" and that it made no sense to him. The Catholic theologian, Aidan Nichols, OP, has asked a key question: *"How can there be an aspect of God not included in the divine essence?"*

Catherine La Cugna noted in a sympathetic account of

Palamism that Palamas was a "poor philosopher" and that the Palamites in their excessive apophatic theology of the Unknowability of God

> do not explain how we KNOW that God's essence is unknowable. If we cannot know the essence of God, then we cannot know that it is an unknowable essence. Nor do the Palamites explain how we KNOW that through the energies we know 'God as such' though not 'God as He is in Himself.'[9]

Other scholars have noted that Palamas lacked a "metaphysics of substance" resulting in much confused terminology. He felt the need to posit a "super-essence" for God but this resulted in the three Persons of the Holy Trinity no longer being "of one substance" with whom man can participate in the divine nature by grace. It is not surprising that his early opponent Barlaam of Calabria observed that if God is communicable in his energies but not in his essence of substance, it follows that his energies are not identical with his essence. There are therefore two Gods, one communicable, and the other, incommunicable.

With regard to the interminable centuries-old controversy between Latins and Greeks regarding the procession of the Holy Spirit, Palamas is seen to deviate in some degree even from the

---

[9] Catherine Morwy La Cugna: *God for Us: The Trinity and Christian Life* (Harper Collins /San Francisco, 1991), 191.

previous Byzantine polemicists who held that the *Holy Spirit proceeded from the Father alone.* According to Palamas, it is not the person of the Holy Spirit who proceeds from the Father but the Holy Spirit as an uncreated divine energy that proceeds from or through the Father *and the Son* (this last an accommodation to the Western doctrine of 'Filioque' but one remaining unacceptable to Catholics). Here again, we see the Holy Spirit regarded as inaccessible to us as belonging to the divine essence. It is painfully evident that Palamas used his real distinction in God as well as his abuse of the Fathers' use of the term 'energy' for a polemic purpose, namely, to explain why the Person of the Holy Spirit could not eternally proceed from or through the Son as the Catholic Church teaches.

It is also interesting that Palamas's modern disciples share Palamas's denial (and that of many of his Byzantine contemporaries) of a Particular Judgment at death wherein the souls of the departed immediately enter Heaven, or undergo a temporary purification in the state called purgatory, or the Hell of the damned. Medieval Byzantine and some Western theologians were influenced by some of the Greek Fathers who were ambiguous in expression concerning the state of souls between death and the Last Judgment or outright postponed the bliss of Heaven for the saved until after the Last Judgment. However, the Latin tradition became more and more explicit concerning,

1. the existence of purgatorial punishments;
2. the just receiving beatitude immediately after death; and

Chapter 3: On Whether Palamism is an Impediment to Reunion

3. that heavenly happiness consisted in the "face-to-face" beatific vision of the Holy Trinity.

For Catholics, Pope Benedict XII's dogmatic pronouncement in "Benedictus Deus" (1336) concerning the beatific vision and the Reunion Council of Florence's dogmatic decree (1439)—which saw both Greek and Latin bishops repudiating false teachings spread concerning purgatory, the Particular Judgment, and the Beatific Vision awarded the just—ended much confusion in these matters. Neo-Palamites, however, reflect the denial and confusion of their Byzantine ancestors in denying the Particular Judgment at death. As one neo-Palamite (Fr. Michael Azkoul) wrote: "There is no soul in heaven or hell." This ostensibly occurs only after the Last Judgment. This is not Catholic doctrine. Unfortunately, most Orthodox continue to deny the existence of the Particular Judgment, delaying divine retribution until after the Last Judgment.

Perhaps the best explanation for Palamas's philosophical errors and consequent flawed theology offered by various scholars is that he read into the ancient Greek Fathers his own confused concepts and categories in order to justify his distinguishing the essence of God from his "uncreated energies." His philosophical language further distinguishing God's "superessential essence" from his essence only created further problems as with his notion of knowable and participable "uncreated energies." Neo-Palamites who in their attacks on Catholic teaching persist in rejecting any "created grace" (blaming St. Augustine for that and other various "heresies") ignore that Palamas himself wrote of "created grace" and even drew (secretly) upon Augustine's famous treatise on the

Trinity.

The Anglican bishop Rowan Williams has commented trenchantly on the linguistic and philosophical problems encountered in reading Palamas's theology:

> Palamas has come to be presented as *the* doctrine of the Eastern Church on the knowledge of God, and any critical questioning of Palamism is interpreted as an attack upon the contemplative and experiential theology of Orthodoxy. However, scholars, by no means unsympathetic to the Eastern tradition, have cast serious doubts upon whether the Palamite distinction of *ousia* from *energeiai* is really a legitimate development of the theology of the Cappadocians or Maximus the Confessor...Against the Eunomian heretics, Basil and the Gregories insist that God's *energeia* are inseparable, the *energeia* is one.... *The patristic defense of Trinitarian dogma points us toward an identification of ousia and energeia.*... Palamism is philosophically a rather unhappy marriage of Aristotelian and Neoplatonic systems; the characteristic extreme realism of Neoplatonic metaphysics coloring (and confusing) a terminology better understood in terms (inadequate though they may be) of the Aristotelian logic already applied to Christian trinitarianism.[10]

---

[10] Williams, Rowan: "The Philosophical Structures of Palamism" in *Eastern Churches Review*, Vol. IX, no. 1-2 (1977); 41.

Chapter 3: On Whether Palamism is an Impediment to Reunion

Contrary to the claims of recent neo-Palamites and other Orthodox, the distinctive tenets of Palamism, cannot (fortunately) be said to constitute dogma. There are Orthodox theologians in the past and present who distanced themselves from key Palamite tenets knowing that the 14th century Councils of Constantinople sanctioning Palamism lack the Ecumenical character for the determination of immutable dogma. There are Orthodox theologians who regard the chief tenets of Palamism not to be dogma but rather *theologumena* (weighty theological opinions). They question the wisdom of Orthodoxy's apparent dogmatization of the real distinction between God's essence and energy. Some Catholic writers believe that if Palamas's essence-energy distinction were merely nominal or metaphorical, it would be reconcilable with Catholic teaching. But as a real distinction placed in the very Being of God, it results in causing and reinforcing fatal doctrinal errors which constitute impediments to the Reunion of the Catholic and Orthodox Churches. The fact remains that the followers of Palamas continue to promote errors which are part of the theological system of Palamism:

1. The denial of the eternal hypostatic Procession of the Holy Spirit from (or through) the Father and the Son;
2. The defense of the existence of "uncreated energies" in God which are "divinities", thereby destroying the Unity of God;
3. The denial that the it is the Person of the Holy Spirit who indwells the souls of the just;
4. The doctrine that one can see with one's bodily eyes in this

life the "uncreated" Light of Tabor;
5. The denial of the reality or possibility of the Beatific Vision and that the just in heaven possess the Beatific Vision of the One and Trine God;
6. The denial of an immediate Particular Judgment at death.
7. The questionable Palamite-hesychastic teaching on grace and insistence on the "felt-experience of God." (Example from a contemporary monk on Mt. Athos: "When man unites with God by grace, he also receives the experience of God, he feels God. For otherwise, how could we unite with God without feeling His grace?"
8. The denial of the universal authority and jurisdiction of the Successor of Peter as "Vicar of Christ" and visible head of the entire Church, East and West. In an explanation of how the 14th century Palamite controversy brought Orthodox ecclesiology into direct conflict with the rise of Papal 'monarchy,' the Greek Old Calendarist Archbishop Chrysostomos of Etna has written:

Whereas for the Palamites, each individual may attain to the status of 'vicar of Christ,' by virtue of his transformation, purification, union with God, and identification by Grace, the Papal monarchy came to claim for the person of the Bishop of Rome alone, and this by virtue of his election to that See, what was for the Orthodox the universal goal of the Christian faith, that criterion of spiritual authority that brought Patriarch and pauper into a oneness of spiritual authority and charismatic power. Here was manifested the collision between Papism and Hesychasm. ...[11]

The above involves a strange replacement of the dogmatic infallibility of the Church. It is no longer centered on the supreme hierarchical authority of the Successor of Peter (united with the Bishops in communion with him) but now exercised by an elite mystical collectivity of Saints who claim to have communion with God through the vision of the Uncreated Light of Tabor. This is simply an incredible perversion of the ecclesiology of the first thousand years. It is to ignore absolutely the teachings of the Fathers, Saints, Ecumenical Councils, and Popes of the First Millennium who testified to the Popes' exercising a juridical and universal supremacy over all the Churches of East and West—one instituted, moreover, by Christ Himself to safeguard the visible Unity of His "one and only" Church built on the Rock of Peter.

---

[11] The Old Calendarist Archbishop Chrysostomos of Etna: Orthodox and Roman Catholic Relations from the Fourth Crusade to the Hesychastic Controversy (2001).

4.

Fr. Coniaris and the Questionable Theology of Gregory Palamas

It should be noted that, contrary to some other Eastern Orthodox writers, including such Orthodox Byzantine theologians as Mark of Ephesus (fifteenth century), Fr. Coniaris agrees with Catholic teaching that a particular or intermediate judgment takes place immediately after one's death.[1] He ignores both Mark of Ephesus, who taught a soul does not receive the sentence of its eternal fate until the General Judgment at the end of time, and the Byzantine Gregory Palamas, who denied that the blessed in heaven see the essence of God in the beatific vision.

However, Fr. Coniaris's teaching reflects other aspects of the theology of Palamas, a fourteenth-century theologian whose view of prayer, which involved a vision-mysticism, resulted in fierce controversies among his fellow Byzantines of that period. Fr. Coniaris observes:

> St. Gregory Palamas came up with a doctrine of God that was shaped entirely by prayer. Not too many of our doctrines have been shaped by prayer as directly as the one by

---

[1] Fr. Anthony M. Coniaris, *Introducing the Orthodox Church: Its Faith and Life* (Minneapolis: Light and Life Publishing, 1982), 110-111.

Palamas.[2]

He accepts Palamas's strange teaching on prayer, in which the theologian argues one can see the divine light of Tabor, a parallel, he says, to the experience Peter, James, and John experienced at the Transfiguration:

> [W]e shall enjoy the open vision of God. "We shall see him as he is" (1 John 3:2). The vision begins on earth. At the Transfiguration, the disciples were able to see the divine light which shone from the Person of Jesus. . . . The Church Fathers tell us that man's purpose in life is to be able to see the divine light as much as we are able. . . . Already in this life the Christians can experience the vision of God. The ascetic Fathers sought to experience this vision of the divine light through prayer and meditation. We call this *theosis* or participation with divine glory. "For now we see in a mirror dimly, but then face to face," says Paul (1 Cor 13:12). Heaven is to be with God "face to face." Our eyes are destined to gaze upon the fullness of God's glory forever.[3]
>
> We find the light of Mount Tabor within ourselves.[4]

The writings of certain spiritual writers who favor such a light-

---

[2] Fr. Coniaris, *Introducing the Orthodox Church*, 200.
[3] Fr. Coniaris, *Introducing the Orthodox Church*, 119.
[4] Fr. Coniaris, *Introducing the Orthodox Church*, 200.

mysticism—for example, Pseudo-Makarios, Symeon the New Theologian, Theophane the Recluse, and also the author of the well-known book *The Way of a Pilgrim*, with its bizarre emphasis on breathing exercises to have "the mind descend into the heart . . . [and] to produce the warm feeling of God's presence within"—are recommended by Fr. Coniaris without the necessary cautions against the danger of spiritual illusion or even delusion. The priest fails to give the theological context developed by Gregory Palamas in support of such "spirituality." For Palamas, this "mind in the heart" is treated as some kind of organ for the perception of an uncreated divine light. For him, the light of the Transfiguration shown on Mount Tabor is really divine and uncreated, and is the energy of God really distinct from God's essence and is capable of being seen in an ecstatic experience. This vision of divine light seen by the ascetics and monks on Mount Athos purportedly brings about the grace of *theosis* or divinization.

In contrast, Catholic doctrine does not accept Palamas's placing a real distinction between God's essence (divine nature) and His energies, nor that there exist in God distinct "uncreated energies." Rather God's essence and energy are identical, and there can be no literal corporeal experience of His essence or energy for "wayfarers," that is, those of here on earth. Nor does Catholic doctrine accept that the light of Tabor was uncreated, or that God can be literally seen—*in his divine essence*—in this life. God is not truly light that can be visibly perceived as the result of "the mind's descent into the heart," and the mind is not to be treated as an organ for experiencing grace. *Theosis* or divinization is not the pinnacle result of the vision of the "uncreated light," but results from living the supernatural life of grace in Christ begun in baptism. It is baptism that brings about our union with God and which makes men a "new creation," that is, "partakers of the divine nature" (2 Pet 1:4). Fr. Coniaris writes that the blessed in heaven will see God "face-to-face," but he neglects to note that, in Gregory Palamas's teaching, it is not the essence of God that will be seen in the beatific vision (as Catholics believe), but rather His "uncreated energies." More could be said concerning the exaggerated ascetic spirituality of Palamas and his Hesychast[5] disciples, and the questionable theology of "essence and uncreated energies" underlying this spirituality, which represents a deviation from classical Byzantine theology and was cultivated by monastic enthusiasts with their desire for visionary experiences. Serious scholars continue to dispute Palamas's doctrine of God, and they point out his having distorted the teachings of the Fathers. Despite the claims of some of his neo-Palamite disciples, it cannot be said that his peculiar theological doctrines constitute dogma among all Eastern Orthodox.

---

[5] Traditional Hesychasm, deriving from the Greek *hesychia* (meaning "holy stillness" or "quietness"), refers to the monastic life as found among the ancient Greek, Coptic, and Syrian Fathers from the third century onward. In his brand of neo-Hesychasm, Palamas also taught that the saints do not see the essence of God but only His "uncreated energies."

5.

The Mariology of Gregory Palamas

Fr. E. G. Farrugia, SJ, longtime professor at the Pontifical Oriental Institute in Rome, has noted perceptively that:

> [I]n Byzantine Orthodoxy, Mariology as a separate field of study does not exist, and yet the veneration of Mary permeates the entire life of the Church and may be said to be a "dimension" of dogma, piety, Christology, and ecclesiology. What we call Mariology as a coherent and sustained effort is no more than the attempt to render this dimension explicit.... It is the Liturgy which provides the main if not exclusive locus of Mariology in the Orthodox Church.... Mariology (according to Fr. Alexander Schmemann) is an attempt to understand the Church from within. If Christ is the icon of the Father, then Mary is the icon of the new creation.[1]

In the writings of later medieval Byzantine spiritual writers, one also finds a striking reaffirmation of the rich Marian doctrines of the Catholic Church, which continue to be splendidly heralded in the doxological liturgical services of the Byzantine Greek Rite

---

[1] Fr. E. G. Farrugia, SJ, *Orientalia Christiana Periodica*, vol. 64 (1998), 534–535.

shared by Catholics and Orthodox.

Gregory Palamas, the fourteenth-century Archbishop of Thessalonica (1296–1359), is regarded as one of the most important theologians and spiritual writers influencing modern Byzantine Greco-Slav theology and spirituality.

It is perhaps an exaggeration to say, as Catherine Mowry LaCugna did in her book *God for Us: The Trinity and Christian Life*, that "Gregory is as central a figure in the East as Thomas Aquinas in the West."[2] But there is no question that Palamas is one of the most important figures for the study of later medieval Byzantine theology and the writers of what may be called the neo-Palamite school of Orthodox theology, which has been given new stature by such Russian Orthodox theologians as Frs. Georges Florovsky and John Meyendorff. Gregory Palamas's peculiar philosophical-theological theses, may be said to stem from his central doctrine of *deification* or *divinization* of the Christian faithful. However, to protect the absolute transcendence of the divine essence, the "theologian of Hesychasm"[3] was to insist on the real distinction he placed between essence (*ousia*) and energies in God. This distinction was understood by the opponents of Palamism,

---

[2] Catherine Mowry LaCugna, *God for Us: The Trinity and Christian Life*, 131.

[3] As noted earlier, traditional Hesychasm derives from the Greek *hesychia* (meaning "holy stillness" or "quietness"). It refers to the monastic life as found among the ancient Greek, Coptic, and Syrian Fathers from the third century onward. In his brand of neo-Hesychasm, Palamas also taught that the saints do not see the essence of God but only His "uncreated energies."

including such Eastern converts to Catholicism as Demetrios Kydones and Manuel Calecas, to deny the simplicity of the Godhead, as well as placing the divine essence of God, that is, the divine nature, beyond the Divine Persons—and the Divine Persons beyond the divine energies. Fierce controversies racked the medieval Byzantine Greek Church, pitting the monastic followers of Palamas and their theological opponents. Byzantine synods in 1341, 1347, and 1351 took place, which approved Palamas's controversial teachings on God's essence and energies, and the "eternal and uncreated divine light" which his fervent supporters among the Hesychastic monks on Mount Athos claimed to be able to see in this life. Nine years after his death at age sixty-three, Palamas was declared a saint by his friend and disciple, the Patriarch of Constantinople Philotheos Kokkinos, and his feast is celebrated on the Second Sunday of Lent in the current Byzantine Orthodox liturgical calendar. Some Orthodox scholars hold Palamas's teachings on the essence and "uncreated energies" of God to constitute dogma, while others only *theologoumena*. In addition, there is analysis showing how Palamite teachings appear incompatible with Catholic doctrine. Suffice it to repeat here Prof. LaCugna's wise observation: "Since the Orthodox claim that Palamism is the normative understanding of Christian faith and experience, the philosophical underpinnings of Gregory's position must be submitted to careful scrutiny."[4] Nevertheless, various aspects of Palamas's ascetical-mystical spirituality, as well as his theology of divinization, which echo the thought of the great Eastern Fathers of the Church, are of

---

[4] LaCugna, *God for Us*, 197.

great value to Catholics, as are aspects of Palamas's rich Mariology. This presentation will be limited to providing but a brief introduction to the sublime Marian doctrine of Palamas, drawing chiefly on his homilies which are available in English. Palamas's homilies, sixty-three of which are extant and most being written between 1347 and 1359, when he served as Archbishop of Thessalonica, reveal the exalted and superlative place of the Mother of God in the plan of salvation. The Greek Orthodox editor of the critical edition of Palamas's collected works, Panagiotis Christou, considered *The Homilies* "one of the most important contributions to Christian literature." Fortunately, the first twenty-one homilies have recently—and superbly—been translated into English and edited by Christopher Veniamin.[5]

Fr. John Meyendorff, who did so much to bring Gregory Palamas's theology and spirituality to the attention of the West and English-speaking peoples, summarized Palamas's doctrine on the *Theotokos*, Mary, the Mother of God:

> Gregory's thought concerning Mary is inspired by an extremely realist view of the divine maternity, expressed by the dogma of [the Ecumenical Council of] Ephesus; the Incarnation of the Word was brought about in her and by her; the person of Christ is therefore inseparable from that of his Mother. When Palamas, following the tradition of the Fathers and, even more, the Liturgy, applies to Mary

---

[5] See The Homilies of Saint Gregory Palamas, vol. 1, (South Canaan, PA: St. Tikhon's Seminary Press, 2002).

adjectives which, biblically, seem reserved for Christ, *he is not thinking of the person of Mary taken by itself and, so to say, statically, but of "her who begat God."* For him, as for the whole tradition of the Church, "Mariology" is one particular and necessary aspect of orthodox Christology which asserts both the full divinity and the full humanity of Christ: without Mary, this union could not have been realized in the person of Jesus.[6]

Drawing on Palamas's rich treasury in *The Homilies*, Fr. Meyendorff proceeded to quote key texts expressive of the Archbishop's Marian teachings:

— [Thus, the Mother of God] is the source and root of the race of liberty.[7]
— [Her body, the temple of God is] the medicine which saves our race.[8]
— Alone, placing herself between God and the whole human race, she made of God a son of man and transformed men into sons of God.[9]
— The Virgin Mary alone dwells on the frontier between created and uncreated natures, and those who know

---

[6] Fr. Meyendorff, *A Study of Gregory Palamas*, 232–233, emphasis added.
[7] Palamas, *The Homilies*, Hom. 14
[8] Palamas, *The Homilies*, Hom. 37.
[9] Palamas, *The Homilies*, Hom. 37.

God recognize also in her the habitation of the infinite.[10]
- [It is from her that] the saints receive all their sanctity.[11]
- No one can come to God except through her.... For it is only through her mediation that He has come to us, that He appeared on earth and dwelt among men.[12]
- [Being thus at the center of salvation, the Virgin is] the cause of events before her time, the leader in the sequence of events thereafter, and the distributor of eternal blessings; she is the thought of the prophets, the chief of the apostles, the prop of the martyrs, and the foundation of the Doctors.... She is the summit of the achievement of all that is holy.[13]
- All divinely inspired Scripture was written for the sake of the Virgin who begat God.[14]
- In addition, she enjoyed the particular privilege of being the first to see the Risen Jesus.[15]
- [The Temple at Jerusalem was the] type [of Mary, for she is the true] place of God.[16]
- [She is] the true throne of the Lord, for there where the King sits, there is his throne.[17]

---

[10] Palamas, *The Homilies*, Hom. 14.
[11] Palamas, *The Homilies*, Hom. 37.
[12] Palamas, *The Homilies*, Hom. 37.
[13] Palamas, *The Homilies*, Hom. 53.
[14] Palamas, *The Homilies*, Hom. 57.
[15] Palamas, *The Homilies*, Hom. 18.
[16] Palamas, *The Homilies*, Hom. 53.
[17] Palamas, *The Homilies*, Hom. 57.

Chapter 5: The Mariology of Gregory Palamas

— The Blessed Mother is the receptacle of the treasure which God granted to men,[18] and the tongs which the seraphim used to take up the live coal which touched the mouth of the prophet Isaiah, prefiguring the Incarnation.[19]

Fr. Meyendorff observed that:

These epithets[20] applied to Mary, for all their rhetorical and lyrical quality, all refer to her part in the Incarnation; *therefore they do not infringe on the worship due to God alone, but rather bear witness to an extremely Christocentric form of piety and conception of history; worship*[21] *of the Mother is indeed addressed to the God-man whom she bore.*

---

[18] Palamas, *The Homilies*, Hom. 53.

[19] Palamas, *The Homilies*, Hom. 14.

[20] "Epithet" typically has negative connotations in modern times. However, as *Webster's Dictionary* notes, "*Epithet* comes to us via Latin from the Greek noun *epitheton* and ultimately derives from *epitithenai*, meaning 'to put on' or 'to add.' In its oldest sense, an epithet is simply a descriptive word or phrase, especially one joined by fixed association to the name of someone or something (as in 'Peter the Great')." See www.merriam-webster.com.

[21] As he makes clear from the whole context, Fr. Meyendorff uses "worship" in a qualified way regarding the Blessed Mother, namely, that she is accorded the special honor of *hyperdulia*, whereas saints in general are venerated via *dulia*, and the Divine Persons alone receive the worship, strictly speaking, of *latria*, the highest expression of which is the Sacrifice of the Mass.

> It is only when one considers that worship outside the precise concept of divine maternity, that one strays beyond the biblical and traditional domain.[22]

Along with other Orthodox theologians, Fr. Meyendorff clearly believed that the Immaculate Conception represented such a "straying beyond the biblical and traditional domain," and presents Palamas as one,

> whose very striking piety with regard to the Virgin would have led him to accept that doctrine, *if he had shared the Western conception of original sin.* . . . Palamas's view of the sin of Adam, and the way in which it was transmitted, cannot be reconciled with the doctrine of the Immaculate Conception as defined by Rome.[23]

Fr. Meyendorff appears correct in his assessment of Palamas's theology, because the "doctor of Hesychastic experience" repeatedly affirmed that Christ alone was immaculately conceived when He took flesh in the womb of the Blessed Virgin. Fr. Meyendorff quotes a text from Palamas's "Homily on the Dormition," wherein he states that the Blessed Virgin *was freed (purified) from original sin at the Annunciation*:

> Palamas asserts that it was at the Annunciation that God

---

[22] Fr. Meyendorff, *A Study of Gregory Palamas*, 232–234, emphasis added.

[23] Fr. Meyendorff, *A Study of Gregory Palamas*, 234, emphasis added.

pronounced "*the very words that made the counterpart to the condemnation of Eve and of Adam . . . and turned it into a benediction.*"[24]

However, in Palamas's writings, there are other puzzling passages that the Blessed Virgin was All-Pure and Holy from the *first moment of her existence*. It is not surprising that such passages would lead some Catholic authors, for example, Fr. Martin Jugie, AA, to think Palamas taught the doctrine of the Immaculate Conception.[25]

As the eminent Byzantinist Fr. Francis Dvornik observed,

[Palamas] must have often meditated on the mystery of the Incarnation and on the purity of the Mother of God. Knowing that nobody is exempt from original sin and unable to imagine how the Word could take flesh from a body stained by sin, he imagined that God had chosen Mary from the beginning and had prepared her sanctity by purifying her ancestors and lastly, Mary herself. . . . He could not accept the idea of God taking his flesh from a body which had been even slightly stained by sin.[26]

---

[24] Palamas, *The Homilies*, Hom. 57.

[25] Fr. Jugie, AA, *L'Immaculée Conception Dans l'Ecriture Sainte et Dans la Tradition Orientale*, 229–230.

[26] "The Byzantine Church and the Immaculate Conception," in The Dogma of the Immaculate Conception, Fr. E. D. O'Connor, CSC, ed., (Notre Dame, IN: University of Notre Dame Press, 1958), 109.

Thus, Palamas did not hesitate to avow that, as a result of the Holy Spirit's *progressive purification* of her ancestors, for example, Seth, Enoch, Lamech, Noah, etc., the Virgin was from the beginning of her life *absolutely sinless* in preparation for giving birth to the All-Pure Son of God. To his mind, she was the Immaculate *yet still not conceived Immaculate,* because only Christ in his view was the result of an immaculate conception, that is, *being conceived by and born of a virgin.* The result of this "progressive purification" was that the person of the Blessed Virgin was not tainted by the "ancestral sin."[27] At the same time, Palamas held that Mary's nature shared with all the descendants of Adam the responsibility for the original transgression by Adam, which meant she also needed a Savior.[28] Clearly, Palamas's teaching contained an internal tension, if not outright contradiction. Writing in 1963, Dom Polycarp Sherwood, OSB, had perceptively remarked:

> True, this purification is attributed to the Spirit; but the progressive purification through the generations must at some point come to the removal of the last vestige of the ancestral sin. Yet how can this be when the very act of procreation conveys the curse and condemnation of the offspring? Nor does Palamas suggest an exception to this rule, save birth without seed. . . . Palamas does not bring the two affirmations—the unique sinlessness of Christ and the

---

[27] Palamas, *The Homilies*, Hom. 52.

[28] As noted earlier, the Catholic Church teaches that Mary experienced redemption in a preservative manner, i.e., prior to her conception, so that she was conceived without sin.

Chapter 5: The Mariology of Gregory Palamas

complete purity of the Virgin—into a stable and theologically understandable relation. . . . Palamas's doctrine appears in a state of incomplete development.[29]

The learned Benedictine indicated that it was the unsatisfactory and incoherent nature of Palamas's teaching on original sin that resulted in his falling short of an explicit belief in the Immaculate Conception of the *Theotokos*, as the Catholic Church would define it. Though Palamas held that the All-Holy Virgin was, in fact, not subject to concupiscence and ignorance, in affirming that Mary was *purified* of original sin, he failed to specify what precisely the ancestors of the Virgin, as well as the Virgin herself, were purified from! It is evident that in affirming Mary was purified of original sin, Palamas stressed an understanding of original sin in terms of its major material effect, namely bodily death. He did not deny that the fall of Adam resulted in the loss of divine life for all his descendants and the transmission of a fallen human nature to all his descendants,[30] but for him the essence of original sin resided in the corruption that was hereditary, namely, in human nature's bondage to death. The All-Holy Virgin, whatever her personal holiness, did not escape the heritage of bodily mortality in her nature, and thus, for Palamas, Mary was conceived in original sin. Here one sees the tendency found in some of the Greek Fathers to emphasize Christ's Redemption as one of redemption from death rather than redemption from sin. Various Catholic scholars have

---

[29] "Byzantine Mariology," Eastern Churches Quarterly, Winter 1962, 384–385.

[30] cf. Palamas, *The Homilies*, Hom. 5, no. 1.

similarly observed that the traditional Greek "theology of grace" was more concerned with man's divinization than his liberation from sin.

In an article "*La Mariologia di Gregorio Palamas*", Fr. Yannis Spiteris, OFM Cap., who later served as the Catholic Archbishop of Corfu, Zante and Cefalonia in Greece, confirms the judgment that Palamas did not teach the doctrine of the Immaculate Conception as Catholics understand it.[31] With other Catholic scholars, he notes that in Palamas's theology of grace and original sin, "not to be conceived in sin is to have been conceived virginally. In this sense, only Christ possessed this privilege."[32]

Similarly, in his larger work, *Palamas, la Grazia e l'esperienza: Gregorio Palamas nella discussion teologica*,[33] Fr. Spiteris noted how Palamas admitted the Blessed Virgin's being conceived in sin *while yet proclaiming her absolute sanctity from the beginning of her existence*. Consider these words: "How can we fail to sing and glorify without cease the Mother of the head of our salvation, of the Giver of Life, in celebrating her conception, her birth and her

---

[31] Fr. Yannis Spiteris, OFM Cap., "La Mariologia di Gregorio Palamas" (Lateranum, n.s., vol. 62, (1996), 553–585.

[32] La Mariologia de Gregorio Palamas," Lateranum, 575.

[33] Fr. Yannis Spiteris, OFM Cap., *Palamas, la Grazia e l'esperienza: Gregorio Palamas nella discussion teologica* (Rome: Lipa Edizione, 1996).

Chapter 5: The Mariology of Gregory Palamas

entry into the holy of holies[34] (the Temple at her Presentation)?"[35]

It was such statements that appeared to some Catholic authors, as remarked previously, to reflect belief in the Catholic doctrine of the Immaculate Conception. But this was to ignore Palamas's flawed theology of original sin. Fr. Spiteris may be said to have summed up well Palamas's thought on the conception of Mary:

> From the moment that Mary was chosen from all eternity and prepared through the series of generations in order to be the worthy tabernacle of the Son of God, giving Him, also from the biological point of view, a pure nature able to unite itself to [her] uncreated purity, when she appeared on earth, she could not have been less than the divine mas-

---

[34] Palamas references here Mary's Presentation in the Temple as a young girl, which is not to be confused with the Presentation of the Baby Jesus in the Temple, which, in turn, is commemorated in the Fourth Joyful Mystery of the Rosary (see Luke 2:22–38).

To be clear, as a young girl, Mary would've entered the Temple in Jerusalem in general, not the holy of holies, the innermost sanctuary of the Temple, where no one but the high priest could enter and he only once each year—on the Day of Atonement (see Lev 16). On that day, the high priest would sprinkle blood on and before the mercy seat of God, which was affixed atop the Ark of the Covenant, and on which God manifested his most intimate presence on earth during the period of the Old Covenant.

However, at the Annunciation, Mary became the Ark of the *New* Covenant, carrying in her womb an even more intimate presence of God on earth: the Incarnate Word, Our Lord Jesus Christ.

[35] Palamas, *The Homilies*, Hom. 52.

terpiece of holiness. Our theologian never tires of describing and singing the praises of this holiness of the Virgin. Faithful to his theological system, Palamas sees in the holiness of Mary two aspects: one, negative, in the sense that she is absolutely without sin; and one, positive, in the sense that she is full of every virtue, but is especially full of the Trinity. . . . Our theologian never tires to call Mary "most holy," "immaculate," "most pure." She was "most pure" even before her birth. Moreover, she received the divine gifts of sanctity beginning from the maternal womb. "God had given Himself to her and her to God even before her birth.". . . If we can refer to the Immaculate Conception of Mary outside the Augustinian schemas of original sin and grace, then we can be in accord . . . with Palamas that truly Mary was the All-Holy one from even the first instance of her existence. For Palamas, Mary was fully divinized by God yet before her birth, because it was for this she was predestined from all eternity. She was not completely conceived in an "immaculate" manner, because she was born as all other men. But it will be she who will bring to birth in an immaculate way, that is, virginally, the Man-God.[36] [37]

---

[36] Palamas, pp. 163, 167.

[37] For a further evaluation of Palamas and the doctrine of the Immaculate Conception, see especially "Letter Forty-Nine" in my book *The Divine Primacy of the Bishop of Rome*, and my article, "An Inadequate Understanding of Original Sin as Source of Eastern Orthodox Objections to the Immaculate Conception," which I've republished in this book as chapter eleven.

Clearly, Palamas's inability to acknowledge that the Blessed Virgin Mary was "free from all stain of original sin" in her conception was due to his defective explanation of original sin. Though he came close to the Catholic formulation of the dogma of the Immaculate Conception, he could not arrive at it since he was hampered by the belief that: 1) the essence of original sin consisted essentially in the mortality of the body, not, as the Catholic Church believes, in the privation of sanctifying or deifying grace resulting in a state of sin; and 2) that the transmission of original sin through sexual intercourse resulted in the infection—and ultimate corruption—of the body by concupiscence, that is, "an inclination" to sin.[38] For Palamas, since the Blessed Virgin Mary was conceived by natural generation of St. Joachim and St. Anne, her body was rendered mortal, thereby sharing in the sinful inheritance affecting all mankind—except, of course, Christ the God-man.

It would also appear Palamas lacked sufficient appreciation for the absolutely gratuitous supernatural elevation of Adam by sanctifying grace, the loss of original justice and holiness resulting in the "spiritual death of the soul" in Adam, and the consequent privation of sanctifying grace to all his descendants. Thus, he failed to grasp that it was because of their solidarity with Adam, the natural head of the human race, that they also *shared in—or contracted—his guilt*.[39] As noted, Palamas also shared with St. Augustine the error wherein "original sin is passed on by the fact of cul-

---

[38] CCC 405–406.
[39] CCC 404.

pable concupiscence intrinsically connected with every conception [resulting from sexual intercourse]."⁴⁰

In another homily,⁴¹ Palamas clearly reveals the influence of St. Augustine's view about the propagation of original sin through sexual reproduction:

> [Christ] was the only one neither sharpen in iniquity nor conceived in sin (cf. Ps 51:5), that is to say, in the fleshly pleasure, passion, and unclean thoughts that belong to our nature defiled by transgression.

Prochoros Kydones, an Athonite monk and one of the leading opponents of Palamas in the Hesychast Controversy that racked the Byzantine Greek Church, took occasion to refute Palamas's views on original justice and original sin.⁴² ⁴³ Like some of his contemporary Western counterparts, Palamas lacked the conceptual insight of Blessed John Duns Scotus, which would have enabled him to envisage the Blessed Virgin's inheriting her human nature in a pure and holy state, having been the subject of an exceptional, privileged grace of *a preservative redemption by the merits of Christ*, which placed her in a state of holiness at her conception.

---

⁴⁰ Fr. Louis Bouyer, Dictionary of Theology, New York: Desclee, 1965, p. 412.

⁴¹ Palamas, *The Homilies*, Hom. 16, no. 5.

⁴² See the sixth book of Kydones's *De Essentia et operatione*, (Vatic. Grec., 1433); only the first two books of this work are found in *PG* t. 151.

⁴³ In addition, like his more famous brother Demetrios Kydones, Prochoros had translated some works of St. Thomas Aquinas.

Chapter 5: The Mariology of Gregory Palamas

Catholics will find much in Palamas's writings to support a "maximalist" theology on the glorious and unique prerogatives of the *Theotokos* and the "hyperdulia" (special devotion) due her. In his book *Theotokos: A Theological Encyclopedia of the Blessed Virgin Mary*,[44] Fr. Michael O'Carroll CSSp reproduced this magnificent quotation from one of Palamas's homilies:

> Today a new world and a wonderful paradise have appeared. In it and from it a new Adam is born to reform the old Adam and renew the whole world. . . . God has kept this Virgin for himself from before all ages. He chose her from among all generations and bestowed on her grace higher than that [given] to all others, making of her, before her wondrous childbirth, the saint of saints, giving her the honours of his own house in the holy of holies. . . . Wishing to create an image of absolute beauty and to manifest clearly to angels and to men the power of his art, God made Mary truly all beautiful. . . . He made of her a blend of all divine, angelic, and human perfections, a sublime beauty embellishing the two worlds, rising from earth to heaven and surpassing even this latter. . . . Must not the one who was to give birth to the fairest of the sons of men have been comparable to Him in everything and been clothed by her Son with marvelous beauty? This Son was, in fact, to resemble her in every aspect so that whoever would see Jesus

---

[44] Fr. Michael O'Carroll CSSp, *Theotokos: A Theological Encyclopedia of the Blessed Virgin Mary* (Wilmington, DE: Michael Glazier, 1983).

would at once recognize, because of this perfect resemblance, the Virgin His Mother.[45]

In Palamas's Homily 52 we read:

The Ever-Virgin, whom we sing and of whom we keep today the festival of her marvelous entry into the holy of holies,[46] we now celebrate. God in fact chose her before all ages in view of the salvation and reestablishment of our race.[47]

Not only for Palamas was the Blessed Virgin predestined from all eternity to be the Mother of God, but she was, in conformity with Eastern tradition, Ever-Virgin, a Virgin before, during, and after the birth of her Divine Son. She suffered no labor pains during the Virgin Birth of Christ, committed no personal sins during her life, and in her dormition died in imitation of her Divine Son, with only a short entombment before her body was assumed to join her soul in heavenly glory. In heaven, she continues to mediate for all mankind. Palamas is profuse in speaking of her as Mediatrix of all Graces:

---

[45] See "Gregory Palamas" in Theotokos, 162.

[46] Again, Palamas references *Mary's* Presentation in the Temple as a young girl, not Our Lord's as an Infant recorded in Luke 2:22–38.

[47] Palamas, Hom. 52, "Preached on the Occasion of the Feast of the Entry of Our Most Pure Queen, the Mother of God, into the Holy of Holies," Eastern Churches Quarterly, Winter 1954–1955, 379.

No divine gifts can reach either angels or men, save through her mediation. As one cannot enjoy the light of a lamp . . . save through the medium of this lamp, so every movement towards God, every impulse towards good coming from Him is unrealizable save through the mediation of the Virgin. . . . She does not cease to spread benefits on all creatures, not only on us men, but on the celestial incorporeal ranks.[48]

His homilies contain more precious testimonies of Palamas's Marian thought:

The Virgin Mother, and she alone, is the frontier between created and uncreated nature. All who know God will recognize her as the one who contained Him who cannot be contained. All who sing hymns to God will praise her next after Him. . . . She is the glory of those on earth, the delight of those in heaven, the adornment of the whole creation. She is the beginning, fount, and root of the hope stored up for us in heaven.[49]

"And the Virgin's name," it says, "was Mary" (Luke 1:27), which means "Lady." This shows the Virgin's dignity, how certain was her virginity and set apart was her life, exact in every respect and completely blameless. She properly bore the name of Virgin, and possessed to the full

---

[48] Fr. O'Carroll, Theotokos: A Theological Encyclopedia, 163.
[49] Palamas, *The Homilies*, Hom. 14, no. 15.

all the attributes of purity. She was a virgin in both body and soul, and kept all the powers of her soul and her bodily senses far above any defilement.[50]

Commenting on the Archangel Gabriel's appearance to the *Theotokos*, Palamas wrote that:

> The Virgin is also duly called "Lady" in another sense, as she has the mastery of all things, having divinely conceived and borne in virginity the Master of all by His nature. Yet she is the Lady not just because she is free from servitude and a partaker of divine power, but because she is the fount and root of the freedom of the human race, especially after the ineffable and joyful birth [of Christ].[51]

When the Blessed Virgin was troubled by the Archangel's words, Palamas writes:

> She was utterly determined to hold fast to her virginity.... The Archangel was not foretelling the future by saying, "The Lord is with thee," but was declaring what he saw happening invisibly at that time. Perceiving that divine and human gifts of grace were to be found in her, and that she was adorned with all the gifts of the Holy Spirit, he truly proclaimed her full of grace. He saw that she had already

---

[50] Palamas, *The Homilies*, Hom. 14, no. 7, "On the Annunciation".
[51] Palamas, *The Homilies*, Hom. 14, no. 8.

received to dwell within her the one in whom are all these treasures of grace. He saw in advance the painless pregnancy and the birth without labour, and announced to her that she should rejoice, and affirmed that she alone was rightly blessed and glorified among women. Even if other women may be extolled, no other can be magnified with the surpassing glory of the Virgin Mother of God.[52]

There is a slight lapse here on the part of Palamas in Homily 14, no. 8. St. Luke makes clear that the Incarnation only took place *after* the Archangel's answer to Mary's question: "How can this happen, since I do not know man?" and *after* her subsequent consent: "Behold the handmaid of the Lord; be it done to me according to thy word" (Luke 1:38; see 1:24–38).

In his magnificent Homily 57, "On the Dormition of Our Supremely Pure Lady *Theotokos* and Ever-Virgin Mary," the Hesychast theologian celebrates in majestic, ecstatic, and sublime terms the Dormition-Assumption of the Mother of God. He calls her the:

Marvel of the whole world [graced with a] surprisingly glorious glory . . . glory for which all mind and word suffice not, though they be angelic. But who can relate those things which came to pass after His ineffable birth? For, as she co-operated and suffered with that exalting condescension (*kenosis*) of the Word of God, she was also rightly glorified and exalted together with Him, ever adding thereto

---

[52] Palamas, *The Homilies*, Hom. 14, no. 8.

the supernatural increase of mighty deeds.

For while she alone stood between God and the whole human race, God became the Son of Man and made men sons of God; she made earth heavenly, she deified the human race, and she alone of all women was shown forth to be a mother by nature and the Mother of God transcending every law of nature, and by her ineffable childbirth—the Queen of all creation, both terrestrial and celestial. . . . But now the Mother of God has her dwelling in heaven whither she was translated, for this is meet, heaven being a suitable place for her. She "stands at the right of the King of all clothed in a vesture wrought with gold and arrayed with divers colors." (cf. Ps 44:9)

For Palamas, in continuing Homily 57, the *Theotokos* was prefigured in the Old Testament. She is "the bush aflame with fire, yet unconsumed" whom Moses beheld. For it was she who conceived and gave birth to "the Divine Fire, Him who takes away the sins of the world." She is "the ark of holiness" (Ps 131:8) who has been resurrected, "ascending from the tomb," and from heaven she "ever cares diligently" for all the faithful and "shows mercy to all." Her station in the Church is one of "preeminence as regards all creatures" and "far transcends that of the celestial hosts":

She only is the frontier between created and uncreated nature, and there is no man that shall come to God except he [who] be truly illuminated through her, that lamp truly radiant with divinity, even as the prophet says, "God is in the midst of her, she shall not be shaken." (Ps 45 [46]:5)

As it was through the Theotokos alone that the Lord came to us, appeared upon earth, and lived among men, being invisible to all before the time, so likewise in the endless age to come, without her mediation, every emanation of illuminating divine light, every revelation of the mysteries of the Godhead, every form of spiritual gift, will exceed the capacity of every created being. She alone has received the all-pervading fulness of Him that fills all things, and through her all may now contain it, for she dispenses it according to the power of each, in proportion and to the degree of the purity of each. Hence, she is the treasury and overseer of the riches of the Godhead. For it is an everlasting ordinance in the heavens that the inferior partake of what lies beyond being by the mediation of the superior, and the Virgin Mother is incomparably superior to all. It is through her that as many partake of God do partake, and as many as know God understand her to be the enclosure of the uncontainable one, and as many hymns praise God praise her together with Him. . . . She is the glory of those upon earth, the joy of celestial beings, the adornment of all creation. She is the beginning and the source and root of unutterable good things; she is the summit and consummation of everything holy.[53]

Regarding the traditional doctrine of Our Lady's being assumed

---

[53] Palamas, *The Homilies*, Hom. 57.

into heaven, body and soul, Palamas argued as theologians in both East and West have done across the centuries:

> How could it be that the body which not only received in itself the pre-eternal and only-begotten Son of God, the ever-flowing wellspring of grace, but also manifested His body by way of birth, should not have also been taken up into heaven? . . . How indeed could that body suffer corruption and turn to earth? How could such a thing be conceivable for anyone who thinks reasonably?[54]

Though Palamas did not formally pose the question debated between Thomists and Scotists as to the motive for the Incarnation, that is, whether Christ would have become incarnate if Adam had not sinned with its catastrophic consequences on his descendants, he clearly favored the Scotist thesis. For example, he declared:

> The pre-eternal, uncircumscribed, and almighty Word and omnipotent Son of God could clearly have saved man from mortality and servitude to the devil without Himself becoming man. He upholds all things by the word of His power and everything is subject to His divine authority (cf. Heb 1:3). According to Job, He can do everything and nothing is impossible for Him (cf. Job 42:2 LXX[55]). The strength of a created being cannot withstand the power of

---

[54] Palamas, *The Homilies*, Hom. 57.
[55] "LXX" refers to the ancient Greek Old Testament.

the creator, and nothing is more powerful than the Almighty. But the Incarnation of the Word of God was the method of deliverance most in keeping with our nature and weakness, and most appropriate for Him who carried it out, for this method had justice on its side, and God does not act without justice.[56]

Conclusion

The English publication of Gregory Palamas's remaining homilies will provide more theological riches that Catholic scholars and others interested can explore, especially regarding the Marian thought of one of the most prolific Byzantine homilists, a man who excelled in celebrating the many glories of Mary. For Fr. Jugie, who did much to attract attention to Palamas's theological system, these homilies "constitute his best title to glory for posterity." With great power and depth, Palamas expounds on the mystery of Mary in the Christological context of the Byzantine liturgical year.[57]

---

[56] Gregory Palamas, *The Homilies*, Hom. 16, no. 1.

[57] A return to the authentic Byzantine tradition, and acquaintance with the positive elements in Gregory Palamas's theological system, would be a valuable corrective to the errors found in the writings of various Eastern Orthodox theologians and writers who deny original sin is a sin of nature resulting from Adam's fall from grace; identify original sin with sinful concupiscence; attribute moral imperfections to the Mother of God; and who make such surprising comments as those encountered in Fr. Anthony M. Coniaris's book *Introducing the Orthodox Church: Its Faith and Life* (1982): "The Orthodox Church believes that

With great eloquence, he delivered the most magnificent panegyrics and eulogies on the holiness of the Mother of God, affirming with theological surety her divine maternity; her absolute sanctity, despite his reservation regarding the Immaculate Conception; her Perpetual Virginity; the "ineffable" Virgin Birth of her Divine Son; her cooperation in the work of Redemption and salvation; her Dormition-Assumption into heaven; her Queenship of angels and men; and her continuing intercession for sinful mankind as universal Mediatrix. Placed between God and the human race, it is from her that stem all the supernatural goods won for mankind by Christ on the Cross. In a daring expression found in Homilies 44, no. 4, and 53, no. 12, Palamas may be said to have summed up his grand Mariological vision of the divinized person of the All-Holy Virgin Mother of God, whose union with Christ was unsurpassed: "*What Christ is by nature, the Virgin is by grace.*"

On reflection, his approach to the mystery of Mary effectively Marianizes every part of theology, above all soteriology. Translated, this means reflection on the role of Mary in the plan of salvation, and based on this logic, necessarily brings a realization of the unique role of Mary on Calvary, and hence also of the Eucharist at the very heart of the Church. For all his faults, Palamas is an effective witness to the Marian character of Catholic theology, to borrow a favorite term of Scotus, and to the antiquity of this concept in the East.

Mary was cleansed of all sin at the Annunciation after she agreed to accept God's offer" (p. 100), and "We do not pray to the *Theotokos* . . . and to saints; rather we ask them to pray for us" (pp. 101, 104).

Appendix I

Catholic Encyclopedia entry by Adrian Fortescue on

Hesychasm

Mystic movement in the Orthodox Church

Hesychasm (Gr., esuchos, quiet): The story of the system of mysticism defended by the monks of Athos in the fourteenth century forms one of the most curious chapters in the history of the Byzantine Church. In itself an obscure speculation, with the wildest form of mystic extravagance as a result, it became the watchword of a political party, and incidentally involved again the everlasting controversy with Rome. It is the only great mystic movement in the Orthodox Church. Ehrhard describes it rightly as "a reaction of national Greek theology against the invasion of Western scholasticism"[1] The clearest way of describing the movement will be to explain first the point at issue and then its history.

I. The Hesychast System

Hesychasts (esuchastes—quietist) were people, nearly all monks,

---

[1] Krumbacher, Byzant. Litt., p. 43.

who defended the theory that it is possible by an elaborate system of asceticism, detachment from earthly cares, submission to an approved master, prayer, especially perfect repose of body and will, to see a mystic light, which is none other than the uncreated light of God. The contemplation of this light is the highest end of man on earth; in this way is a man most intimately united with God. The light seen by Hesychasts is the same as appeared at Christ's Transfiguration. This was no mere created phenomenon, but the eternal light of God Himself. It is not the Divine essence; no man can see God face to face in this world (John, 1:18), but it is the Divine action or operation. For in God action (enerleia, actus, operatio) is really distinct from essence (ousia). There was a regular process for seeing the uncreated light; the body was to be held immovable for a long time, the chin pressed against the breast, the breath held, the eyes turned in, and so on. Then in due time the monk began to see the wonderful light. The likeness of this process of auto-suggestion to that of fakirs, Sunnyasis, and such people all over the East is obvious.

Hesychasm then contains two elements, the belief that quietist contemplation is the highest occupation for men, and the assertion of real distinction between the divine essence and the divine operation. Both points had been prepared by Greek theologians many centuries before. Although there was comparatively little mysticism in the Byzantine Church, many Greek Fathers and theologians had maintained that knowledge of God can be obtained by purity of soul and prayer better than by study. The quotations made by Hesychasts at the councils (see below) supply many such texts. Clement of Alexandria was most often invoked for this axiom. Pseudo-Dionysius seems to have brought the statement a step nearer to Hesychasm. He describes a medium in which God may be contemplated; this medium is a mystic light that is itself half darkness. But it was Simeon, "the new theologian" (circa 1025 – circa 1092),[2] a monk of Studion, the "greatest mystic of the Greek Church,"[3] who evolved the quietist theory so elaborately that he may be called the father of Hesychasm. For the union with God in contemplation (which is the highest object of our life) he required a regular system of spiritual education beginning with baptism and passing through regulated exercises of penance and asceticism under the guidance of a director. But he had not conceived the grossly magic practices of the later Hesychasts; his ideal is still enormously more philosophical than theirs. There seems also to have been a strong element of the pantheism that so often accompanies mysticism in the fully developed Hesychast system. By contemplating the uncreated light one became united with God so intimately that one became absorbed in Him. This suspicion of pantheism (never very remote from neo-Platonic theories) is constantly insisted on by the opponents of the system.

The other element of fourteenth-century Hesychasm was the famous real distinction between essence and attributes (specifically one attribute—energy) in God. This theory, fundamentally opposed to the whole conception of God in the Western Scholastic

---

[2] See Krumbacher, *op. cit.*, 152–154.
[3] Loc. cit.

system, had also been prepared by Eastern Fathers and theologians. Remotely it may be traced back to Neo-Platonism. The Platonists had conceived God as something in every way unapproachable, remote from all categories of being known to us. God Himself could not even touch or act upon matter. Divine action was carried into effect by demiurges, intermediaries between God and creatures. The Greek Fathers (after Clement of Alexandria mostly Platonists) had a tendency in the same way to distinguish between God's unapproachable essence and His action, energy, operation on creatures. God Himself transcends all things. He is absolute, unknown, infinite above everything; no eye can see, no mind conceive Him. What we can know and attain is His action. The foundation of a real distinction between the unapproachable essence (ousia) and the approachable energy (enerleia) is thus laid. For this system, too, the quotations made by Hesychasts from Athanasius, Basil, Gregory, especially from Pseudo-Dionysius, supply enough examples. The Hesychasts were fond of illustrating their distinction between God's essence and energy (light) by comparing them to the sun, whose rays are really distinct from its globe, although there is only one sun. It is to be noted that the philosophic opponents of Hesychasm always borrow their weapons from St. Thomas Aquinas and the Western Schoolmen. They argue, quite in terms of Latin Aristotelean philosophy, that God is simple; except for the Trinity there can be no distinctions in an actus purus. This distinct energy, uncreated light that is not the essence of God, would be a kind of demiurge, something neither God nor creature; or there would be two Gods, an essence and an energy. From one point of view, then, the Hesychast controversy may be conceived as an issue between Greek Platonist philosophy and Latin rationalist Aristoteleanism. It is significant that the Hesychasts were all vehemently Byzantine and bitter opponents of the West, while their opponents were all latinizers, eager for reunion.

II. History of the Controversy

The leaders of either side were Palamas the Hesychast and Barlaam, from whom the other side is often called that of the Barlaamites. Gregory Palamas (d. about 1360)[4] was a monk at Athos, then from 1349 Bishop of Thessalonica. He wrote no less than sixty works in defense of Hesychasm, one especially against the Scholastic identification of God's essence and attributes. He found fifty heresies in his opponents. He was also vehemently anti-Latin, wrote a refutation of John Beccus's latinizing work, and did his duty by Orthodoxy in supplying the usual treatise against the double procession of the Holy Ghost. Naturally his opponents call him a ditheist, while he considers them Arians, Sabellians, and Epicureans. Barlaam,[5] his chief adversary, was a monk from Calabria who came to Constantinople in the reign of Andronicus III (1328-1341). At first he opposed the Latins, but eventually he wrote in defense of reunion, of the Filioque, and the papal primacy. In 1348 he left Constantinople and became Bishop of Gerace in Calabria.

---

[4] Krumbacher, *op. cit.*, 103–105.
[5] Krumbacher, *op. cit.*, 100

The date of his death is unknown. It was from this Barlaam that Petrarch learned Greek. Gregory Akindynos, a friend and contemporary of Barlaam, also a monk, wrote a work against the Hesychasts "Peri ousias kai enerleias," in six books, of which the first two are nothing but translations from St. Thomas's "Summa contra Gentiles." Nicephorus Gregoras,[6] the historian (d. after 1359), was also one of the chief opponents of Hesychasm. He came to the emperor's court as a young man, was educated by the most famous scholars of that time—the Patriarch John Glycus (John XIII, 1316-1320), and the Great Logothete Theodorus Metochites, and became himself perhaps the most distinguished man of learning in the Greek world of the fourteenth century. He wrote theology, philosophy, astronomy, history, rhetoric, poetry, and grammar. His best-known work is a Roman history in thirty-seven books, describing the period from 1204 to 1329. In the midst of so many occupations he made the acquaintance of Barlaam, and entered the lists with him against Palamas and the Hesychasts. He wrote a number of controversial works to confute these people, and tells the story of the quarrel in his history,[7] with much animus against them. Like most of the anti-Hesychasts Gregoras was a pronounced latinizer. At the time when Barlaam was opposed to the Latins Gregoras wrote against him; with Palamas too he discussed

---

[6] Ibid., 101, 293-298.

[7] Nicephorus Gregorus, *Byzantine History*, volumes. XV, XVIII, XIX, XXII.

the question of reunion with the West in a friendly and conciliatory way. Eventually Gregoras fell into disfavor with the Court and disappeared.

The monks of Athos might have contemplated their uncreated light without attracting much attention, had not the question become mixed up with the unending Latin controversy and with political issues. They had already practiced their system of auto-suggestion for a long time when Barlaam, arriving at Constantinople, began to denounce it as superstitious and absurd. There had been some opposition before. People had heard Palamas boast that he could see the light of God with his eyes, and had accused him of blasphemy; but, since Isaias, the Patriarch of Constantinople (1323–1334), was himself a monk of Athos and a disciple of Palamas, the opposition had not been very successful. However, from the year 1339, when Barlaam arrived in the city, began the really serious quarrel which for twenty years was to rend Orthodox theology, cause enormous commotion at Constantinople, Athos, and all the great centers of the Orthodox world, and lead even to active persecution., Barlaam, like all opponents of Hesychasm, based his objections mainly on a vehement denial of the possibility of an uncreated light that was yet not God's essence; throughout the controversy he and his party used the arguments they had learned in the West to show the impossibility of such distinctions in God. He also made bitter mockery of what he calls the Omphalopsuchia of the monks who sit with bent heads gazing at their own person, and brought various accusations against Palamas's life and manners.

After Isaias, John XIV (John Aprenus, 1334–47) had become patriarch. Barlaam demanded of him a synod to settle the question. For a time, the patriarch refused to take the matter so seriously; eventually, since the quarrel became more and more bitter, in 1341 the first synod of the Hesychast question was summoned at Constantinople. The emperor (Andronicus III) presided. This first synod considered only two questions: (I) Whether the light of Tabor (that of the Transfiguration) was created or not; (2) a certain prayer used by Hesychasts, stated by Barlaam to contain ditheism. The enormous influence of the monks at Court and the want of energy of the patriarch (who was in his heart on Barlaam's side) made this first synod a victory for Hesychasm. In both points the monks and their theory were approved, and Barlaam was forced to withdraw his accusations. Soon afterwards he left Constantinople forever; his cause was taken up by Gregory Akindynos. The emperor died a few days after the synod. John VI, Cantacuzenus (1341–1355), who gradually usurped the imperial power, first as rival, then as fellow-emperor, of Andronicus's son John V, Palaeologus (1341-76), was always a friend of Palamas and the Hesychast monks. The second Hesychast synod under Cantacuzenus, but without the patriarch, condemned Akindynos and introduced a new element by representing him and all its opponents as latinizers who were trying to destroy Orthodoxy.

In 1345 the patriarch summoned the third synod. By now he had definitely made up his mind to withstand the Hesychasts. This synod then, under his. direction, excommunicated Palamas and Isidore Buchiras, Bishop elect of Monembasia in Thessaly, one of

Palamas's disciples. Buchiras and Palamas withdrew their heresy outwardly, and waited for a better chance. The chance came in 1347. By this time their protector John Cantacuzenus had entered Constantinople in triumph and had been crowned emperor. The other party (that of the child-emperor John Palaeologus and of his mother Ann of Savoy) was now helpless. The controversy from this time is complicated by a political issue. Cantacuzenus and his friends were Hesychasts; the party of the Palaeologi were Barlaamites. As long as Cantacuzenus triumphed the Hesychasts triumphed with him; by the time he fell Hesychasm had become so much identified with the cause of the Orthodox Church against the Latins that the other side never succeeded in ousting it. On February 2, 1347, the fourth Hesychast synod was held. It deposed the patriarch, John XIV, and excommunicated Akindynos. Isidore Buchiras, who had been excommunicated by the third synod, was now made patriarch (Isidore I, 1347-1349). In the same year (1347) the Barlaamites held the fifth synod, refusing to acknowledge Isidore and excommunicating Palamas. From this time Nicephorus Gregoras becomes the chief opponent of Hesychasm. Isidore I died in 1349: the Hesychasts replaced him by one of their monks, Callistus I (1350-1354). In 1351 the sixth synod met in the Blachernae palace under Cantacuzenus. Gregoras defended his views boldly and skillfully, but again the Hesychasts had it all their own way, deposed Barlaamite bishops, and used violence against their own opponents. In this synod six questions about God's essence and attributes were answered, all in the Hesychast sense, while Palamas was declared to be without any doubt orthodox and unimpeachable. The synod finally published, in defense of Palamas and his views, a decree (Tomos) which eventually was looked upon as an authentic declaration of the Orthodox Church. From this time Hesychasm may be said to have defeated all opposition. Gregoras was arrested and kept in custody in his own house. He was not set free till Cantacuzenus (with whom rests the eternal disgrace of having first invited the Turks to Europe) was deposed and the Palaeologi triumphed in 1354. Cantacuzenus then withdrew to Athos, became a monk himself, taking the name of Joasaph, and spent the rest of his life writing a history of his own times and contemplating the uncreated light. This history in four books[8] covers the period from 1320 to 1356, and tells the whole story of the Hesychast controversy. Being written by a violent partisan, it forms an interesting contrast to that of Gregoras.

After the deposition of Cantacuzenus, the Barlaamites held an anti-Hesychast synod at Ephesus; but the patriarchs of Constantinople and the great mass of the people had by now become too firmly persuaded that the cause of Hesychasm was that of Orthodoxy. To oppose it was to incur the guilt of latinizing; so even Cantacuzenus's fall was not enough to turn the scale. Hesychasm from this time is always triumphant. About 1360 Palamas died. In 1368 the seventh Synod of Constantinople (concerning this matter) under the Patriarch Philotheus (1364-1376: Callistus's successor) excommunicated the Barlaamite monk Prochorus Cydonius, confirmed the "Tomus" of 1351 as a "Faultless Canon of the true faith

---

[8] In *Migne, PG*, CLIII, CLIV.

of Christians", and canonized Palamas as a Father and Doctor of the Church. So by the end of the fourteenth century Hesychasm had become a dogma of the Orthodox Church. It is so still. The interest in the question gradually died out, but the Orthodox still maintain the Tomus of 1351 as binding; the real distinction between God's essence and operation remains one more principle, though it is rarely insisted on now, in which the Orthodox differ from Catholics. Gregory Palamas is a saint to them. They keep his feast on the second Sunday of Lent and again on November 14.[9] The office for this feast was composed by the Patriarch Philotheus. In the nineteenth century there was among the Orthodox a certain revival of interest in the question, partly historical, but also speculative and philosophical. Nicodemus, a monk of Athos, defended the Hesychasts in his (1801); Eugenius Bulgaris and others, especially Athos monks, have again discussed this old controversy; it is always evident that their theology still stands by the Tomus of 1351, and still maintains the distinction between the Divine essence and energy.

There was a very faint echo of Hesychasm in the West. Latin theology on the whole was too deeply impregnated with the Aristotelean Scholastic system to tolerate a theory that opposed its very foundation. That all created beings are composed of actus and potentia, that God alone is actus purus, simple as He is infinite—this is the root of all Scholastic natural theology. Nevertheless one or two Latins seem to have had ideas similar to Hesychasm. Gilbertus

---

[9] Nilles, "Kalendarium manuale", Innsbruck, 1897, II, 124-125.

Porretanus (de la Porree, d. 1154) is quoted as having said that the Divine essence is not God—implying some kind of real distinction; John of Varennes, a hermit in the Diocese of Reims (c. 1396), said that the Apostles at the Transfiguration had seen the Divine essence as clearly as it is seen in heaven. About the same time John of Brescain made a proposition: *Creatam lucem infinitam et immensam esse.* But these isolated opinions formed no school. We know of them chiefly through the indignant condemnations they at once provoked. St. Bernard wrote to refute Gilbert de la Porree; the University of Paris and the legate Odo condemned John of Brescain's proposition. Hesychasm has never had a party among Catholics. In the Orthodox Church the controversy, waged furiously just at the time when the enemies of the empire were finally overturning it and unity among its last defenders was the most crying need, is a significant witness of the decay of a lost cause.

— Adrian Fortescue

Appendix II

Extract from International Theological Commission document:

Theology, Christology, Anthropology

Section E.

The Image of God in Man, or the Christian Meaning of the "Deification" of Man

1. "The Word of God is made man, that man may become God."[1] This axiom of the soteriology of the Fathers, above all of the Greeks, is denied in our own times for various reasons. Some assert that "deification" is a typically Hellenistic notion of salvation and is conducive to a mentality of flight from the world, together with a denial of human values. In their view deification removes the difference between God and man and leads to a fusion without distinction. They oppose to this patristic axiom another that they maintain is more adapted to our age: "God is made man, so that man may be made more human." Certainly the words "deification", *theôsis*, *theopoiêsis*, *homoiôsis theo*, etc., of themselves

---

[1] Athanasius, *De inc.* 54, 3

are ambiguous. Therefore the genuine or Christian sense of "deification" in its major aspects must be explained.

2. Certainly Greek philosophy and religion acknowledged some "natural" kinship between the human and the divine mind. The biblical revelation, however, clearly treats man as a creature, who by contemplation and love moves toward God. It is not man's intellectual capacity but conversion of heart, a new obedience, and moral action that bring man closest to God. This is impossible without God's grace. Man can become what God is only by grace.

3. Stronger arguments arise from Christian preaching. Created in the image and likeness of God, man is called to a sharing of life with God, who alone can fulfill the deepest desires of the human heart. The idea of deification reaches its summit by virtue of the Incarnation of Jesus Christ. The Word assumes our mortal nature so that we can be freed from death and sin and can share in the divine life. Through Jesus Christ we are partakers in the divine nature (2 Pet 1:4). Deification consists in the very grace that frees us from the death of sin and communicates to us the divine life itself. We are sons in the Son.

4. The Christian meaning of our proposition is made much more profound through the mystery of Jesus Christ. Just as the Incarnation of the Word does not change the divine nature, in the same way the divinity of Jesus Christ does not change or dissolve human nature but rather makes it more itself and perfects it in its original

condition of creaturehood. Redemption does not, in a general way, simply convert human nature into something divine but renews human nature along the lines of the human nature of Jesus Christ.

According to Maximus the Confessor, this idea is further determined through the final experiences of Jesus Christ, namely, his Passion and his abandonment by God. The more deeply Jesus Christ participates in human mystery, the more man participates in the divine life.

In this sense deification properly understood can make man perfectly human: deification is the truest and ultimate hominization of man.

5. This process whereby man is deified does not take place without the grace of Jesus Christ, which comes especially through the sacraments in the Church. The sacraments join us in a most efficacious and visible fashion, and under the symbols of our own fragile life they join us to the divine grace of the Savior.[2] More than that, this deification is not communicated to the individual as such but as a member of the Communion of Saints. Moreover, the invitation given by divine grace to the human race takes place in the Holy Spirit. Christians therefore should realize the holiness they have achieved in their way of life.[3] The fullness of deification belongs to the beatific vision of the Triune God, which takes the soul into the Communion of Saints.

---

[2] Cf. Vatican II, *Lumen Gentium*, 7.
[3] Vatican II, *Lumen Gentium*, 39–42.

Appendix III

Note on the Theology of Gregory Palamas

By Yves Congar

We must now turn to a very important subject which would call for a much more developed treatment if I were to deal with it as such. As regards the theme of this book, it is necessary to speak about Palamite theology, but it is sufficient to do so relatively succinctly. I have, in this, made considerable use of the many indispensable texts and excellent analyses available.[1]

---

[1] D. Stiernon has published a bulletin containing 303 items on Palamism in *Rev. Et. Byz.* 30 (1972), 231–341. This alone shows that the subject is so full and technical that only specialists can deal adequately with it. For the works of Palamas, see J. Meyendorff, *Introduction à l'étude de Grégoire Palamas* (*Patristica Sorbonensia*, 3) (Paris, 1959), Appendix I, pp. 331–399 [the Eng. tr. (see below) lacks the Appendixes]. For our particular subject, only the following need to be consulted: *PG* 150, 809–828: *Chapters against Akindynos*; 909–960: dialogue *Theophanes*; 1121–1126: *Capita CL physica, theologica, moralia et practica*; 1225–1236: *Hagioritic Tome*; *PG* 151, 424-449: *Homilies* 34 and 35 on the Transfiguration and the Light of Tabor; see also J. Meyendorff, ed., *Pour la défense des saints hésychastes* (*Spicil. Sacr. Lov.*, 29) (Louvain, 1959; 2nd ed. 1973). Studies and analyses of Palamas include: I. Hausherr, "La méthode d'oraison hésychaste," *Or. Chr. Period.* 9 (1927), 97–210; M. Jugie, "Palamas et Palamite (Controverse)," *DTC*, XI (1932), cols 1735–

1776, 1777–1818; idem, *Theologia dogmatica Christianorum Orient. ab Ecclesia cath. diss.*, II (Paris, 1933), pp. 47–183; S. Guichardan, *Le problème de la simplicité divine en Orient et en Occident aux XIVe et XVe siècles. Grégoire Palamas, Duns Scot, Georges Scholarios* (Lyons, 1933); B. Krivocheine, "The Ascetic and Theological Teaching of St Gregory Palamas," *ECQ*, 3 (1938–1939), 26–33, 71–84, 138–156, 193–215; V. Lossky, *The Mystical Theology of the Eastern Church* (Eng. tr.; London, 1957), especially pp. 67ff.: "Uncreated Energies"; *idem*, "The Procession of the Holy Spirit in the Orthodox Triadology" (Eng, tr.), *ECQ*, 7, Supplementary Issue (1948), 31-53, also tr. in *In the Image* . . . (see below), chapter 4, pp. 71-96: "The Procession of the Holy Spirit in Orthodox Trinitarian Doctrine": *idem, In the Image and Likeness of God* (Eng. tr., London and Oxford, 1975), especially chapter 3: "The Theology of Light in the Thought of St Gregory Palamas"; C. Lialine, "The Theological Teaching of Gregory Palamas on Divine Simplicity," *ECQ*, 6 (1946), 266–287; C. Kern, "Les éléments de la théologie de Grégoire Palamas," *Irénikon*, 20 (1947), 6–33, 164–193; J. Meyendorff, *A Study of Gregory Palamas* (Eng, tr. of *Introduction, op. cit.*; London, 1964): an original and fundamental work, and, at a less technical level, but more synthetic, *S. Grégoire Palamas et la mystique orthodoxe* (Coll. *Les Maitres spirituels*) (Paris, 1959); *idem*, "the Holy Trinity in Palamite Theology," *Trinitarian Theology: East and West* (Brookline, Mass., 1977), pp. 25–43; E. Boularand, "Grégoire Palamas et 'La Défense des saints hésychastes,'" *RAM*, 36 (1960), 227–240; O. Clément, *Byzance et le Christianisme* (Paris, 1964): R. Miguel, "Grégoire Palamas, docteur de l'expérience," *Irénikon*, 37 (1966), 227–237; Amphilokios Radovic, "'Le Filioque' et l'énergie incréée de la Sainte Trinité selon la doctrine de S. Grégoire Palamas," *Messager de l'Exarchat du Patriarche russe en Europe occidentale*, 89–90 (1975), 11–44; Kallistos Ware, "Dieu caché et révélé. La voie apophatique et la distinction essence-énergie," *ibid.*, 45–59. A double number of the journal *Istina* on "Orient et Occident. La Procession du Saint-Esprit" appeared in 1972 and a series of articles on Gregory Palamas in 1974, of which the

Appendix III: Note on the Theology of Gregory Palamas

Gregory Palamas (1296-1359) became a monk on Mount Athos about 1316 and there experienced Hesychastic spirituality, in which the body is very closely associated with the spirit in the search for recollection and concentration. In Hesychastic prayer, a breathing technique is used to enable the prayer to descend from the head and find its way to the heart. The particular prayer used is the "Jesus Prayer": the words "Lord Jesus Christ, Son of God, have mercy on me" are said again and again in time with the breathing until they become a continuous prayer of the heart. Hesychasm eventually fitted into the pattern of Church and social life of the empire and became a reforming movement, working for the humble and the poor and for the independence and transcendence of the Church.

---

editorial, 257–259, is especially valuable; see also in that number (19) J. P. Houdret, "Palamas et les Cappadociens," 260–271; J.-M. Garrigues, "L'énergie divine et la gráce chez Maxime le Confesseur," 272–296; J.S. Nadal, "La critique par Akindynos de l'herméneutique patristique de Palamas," 297–328; M. J. Le Guillou, "Lumière et charité dans la doctrine palamite de la divinisation," 329–338. The articles in this number of *Istina*, together with several other publications, give the impression of being a combined attack. For a Catholic reply, see A. de Halleux, "Palamisme et tradition," *Irénikon*, 48 (1975). 479–493. Finally, for the epistemological debate, see G. Podskalsky, *Theologie und Philosophie in Byzanz. Der Streit um die theologische Methodik in der spätbyzantinischen Geistesgeschichte (14./15. Jahrhundert), seine systematischen Grundlagen und seine historische Entwicklung* (*Byzantinisches Archiv*, 15) (Munich, 1977), which contains an exhaustive documentation and a full bibliography. See also, footnotes 15 to 20, for Palamas and the Fathers, and footnote 22 for the reception by Catholic theologians of Palamism.

In the meantime, a monk from Calabria, Barlaam, attacked the Hesychasts' claim that it was possible to know God, their practice of prayer, and their theology of the divine light of Mount Tabor. Palamas replied to these attacks, and his defense of the Hesychastic positions forms the basis of Palamite theology. Two synods took place in 1341. Barlaam's teachings were condemned by the first in June and those of Akindynos by the second, which met in August. Despite the approval of these synods, Palamas became involved in the vicissitudes of ecclesiastical politics which led at times to his being excommunicated and the triumph of his enemies and at other times to the confirmation of his teachings. In 1347 he was made Archbishop of Thessalonica, but did not take up his see until 1350. Years of struggle and frequently dramatic episodes followed. He died on 14 November 1359 and was canonized by the Church of Constantinople in 1368. His teaching had by this time already been approved, by a council that met in 1351.[2]

Palamas was almost completely forgotten for several centuries—so much so that T. de Régnon published his four great volumes in 1892-1898 without even referring to him, even in those passages where he was commenting on the term "energy" (IV, pp. 425ff., 476ff.). In the 1930's and 40's, however, there was a wonderful revival of interest in him and his theology. Broadly speaking, Eastern theologians have come to recognize in Palamism a clear expression of the genius and the tradition of their Church. It is therefore of great importance for the theme of this book. It is

---

[2] J. Meyendorff, *A Study, op. cit.*, pp. 94–97; for the text see *PG* 151, 717–762.

also relatively simple. In the first place, there is the whole context of Eastern apophatism, according to which it is not possible either to know God or to express any positive idea of him, the deepest knowledge of him being purely experiential or mystical. At the same time, God calls us to become deified. This is such a fundamental datum in the teaching of the Greek Fathers that they constantly used it as proof of the divinity of the Son and the Spirit in their controversy with the Arians. It is within this context that should be placed the Hesychastic experience of communion with God and of a knowledge, through experience, of his light. According to the Greek tradition, then, there is, in God, a secret essence that cannot be known or shared and a radiation which, once it has been experienced and shared, ensures our deification. This accounts for the distinction that Palamas makes *in God*—without impairing the simplicity of God—not only between the essence and the hypostases, but also between the hypostases, the divine essence that cannot be known or shared, and the uncreated energies of God. These energies are God, not in his being in himself, which is not accessible to creatures, but in his being for us. The energies must be available for us to share in them, and they must be God as uncreated, or else we could never be deified. The Palamists are unable to accept that the created grace of the Scholastic theologians of the West and the intentional union of the Thomists, the depth and realism of which they do not fully understand, can bring about a true deification of man, and the direct vision of the divine essence without any created species, as affirmed by Thomas Aquinas, is, in their view, contrary to the unknowable character of that essence. These uncreated energies are therefore what surround the essence of God that cannot be communicated to man—*ta peri auton* (or *autou*).³

Scriptural terms for these are, for example, the glory, the face, or the power of God. The light that transfigured Christ on Mount Tabor was the uncreated splendour that emanates from God. It was always with Christ because of his divinity, but it remained invisible to carnal eyes—the apostles were only able to perceive it miraculously because their bodily eyes were illuminated by grace. This perception of the divine light is, in the opinion of the Hesychasts and the Palamists, the peak of all spiritual experience, and this idea is very closely associated with the very fundamental decision not to separate the body from the highest spiritual life. What, then, is the relationship between these energies and the hypostases or Persons of the Trinity? According to Sergey Bulgakov, "Palamas hardly touches on the complex and important question of the relationship between the energies and the hypostases (except in a few isolated sentences that are lacking in precision)."⁴

The texts and the studies that have been published since Bulgakov said this enable us to make a better reply to our question. The divine energies are "inhypostatized."⁵ The eternal and uncreated activity that flows from the divine essence is possessed,

---

³ See footnotes 19 and 20.

⁴ S. Bulgakov, *Le Paraclet* (Paris, 1946), p. 236.

⁵ See J. Meyendorff, ed., *Pour la défense des saints hésychastes, op. cit.* (footnote 1), III, 1, 18, Pp. 591–593.

Appendix III: Note on the Theology of Gregory Palamas 113

put to work and manifested by the divine Persons and communicated by them to our persons.⁶ The energetic manifestations of God follow the order (*taxis*) of the Persons—from the Father, through the Som, in the Spirit.

In the particular case of the Holy Spirit, the part played by the latter in the economy of salvation was made manifest at Pentecost, when, however, no incarnation of the hypostasis of the Spirit or communication of the essence of God took place. But the manifestation of his Person by the energies confirms a dependence with regard to the Son. "The grace is therefore uncreated and it is what the Son gives, sends and grants to his disciples; it is not the Spirit himself, but a deifying gift which is an energy that is not only uncreated, but also inseparable from the Holy Spirit." (Triad, III, 8)

At this point Palamas goes back to a statement by Gregory of

---

⁶ J. Meyendorff, *A Study, op. cit.* (footnote 1), pp. 216ff.; *idem*, "The Holy Trinity in Palamite Theology," *op. cit.* (*ibid.*), 31–33, 38–39, in which the author quotes an article by Edmund Hussey, "The Persons-Energy Structure in the Theology of St Gregory Palamas," *St Vladimir's Theological Quarterly*, 18 (1974), 22–43. In this context, it is also worth quoting from O. Clément, *Byzance et le Christianisme, op. cit.* (footnote 1), p. 46: "This energy is not an impersonal radiation subsisting in itself. It is rather an expansion of the Trinity and expresses *ad extra* the mysterious otherness of the Trinity in its unity. It is a 'natural procession' from God himself, bursting or flashing out, like a flash of light, of the Father through the Son and in the Holy Spirit. It reveals the 'interpenetration' or perichoresis of the divine Persons, who 'interpenetrate each other in such a way that they possess only one Energy.'" See also A. de Halleux, "Palamisme et Scolastique," *op. cit.* (footnote 22), 425, who refers to Palamas, *Capita CL physica, op. cit.* (note 1), 75 and 107 (*PG* 150, 1173B and 1193B).

Cyprus, the Patriarch of Constantinople (†1290),[7] and recognizes that the Filioque may possibly have a meaning in the order of energetic manifestation, that is, that the Holy Spirit, not as hypostasis but as inhypostatizing the energy, is poured out from the Father, through the Son (*dia tou Huiou* or even *ek tou Huiou*). Vladimir Lossky discovered this openness as early as 1945, but he kept to the idea of an eternal manifestation of the Spirit through the Son.[8] His disciple O. Clément, however, went further than this and said:

> If the "monarchic" character of the Father as the unique principle of the Son and the Spirit is an absolutely incom-

---

[7] Gregory's treatise on the *exporeusis* of the Holy Spirit (*PG* 142, 269–300) has been analysed by O. Clément, "Grégoire de Chypre 'De l'ekporèse du Saint-Esprit,'" *Istina*, 17 (1972), 443–456.

[8] V. Lossky, "The Procession of the Holy Spirit," *ECQ*, *op. cit.* (footnote 1), 48–49; *In the Image and Likeness of God*, *op. cit.* (ibid.), pp. 90–93. In his article "Vladimir Lossky, un théologien de la personne et du Saint-Esprit (Mémorial Vladimir Lossky), *Messager de l'Exarchat du Patriarche russe en Europe occidentale*, 30–31 (April–September, 1959), 137–206, O. Clément referred to this openness on Lossky's part and, on pp. 192 and 178, points to expressions of it, taken from classes given on 10 November and 17 November 1955: "The *Filioque* can be justified at the level of manifestation—the Holy Spirit manifests the common nature of the Trinity and proceeds from the Father and the Son not as a Person, but as a function. His function is essentially to make manifest. He manifests the nature of the Father and the Son (which is also his own)"; "In this *taxis* (of manifestation), it is possible to say, if need be, that the Spirit proceeds from the Father and the Son. The Son shows in himself what the Father is; the Spirit shows what the Father is and what the Son is, insofar as they are the same principle, but a principle to which the Spirit himself belongs and which he manifests."

municable hypostatic character, is his character as the divine source (of the essence and energies) to use a Latin theological term, his "fontal" privilege—not communicated to the Son and then from the Father and the Son to the Spirit, the source of our deification? And would it not be this participation in the divine source, the rhythm that makes first the Son and then the Spirit the source with the Father, that is indicated by a certain Latin (and Alexandrian) Filioque?[9]

It may be because I am not sufficiently well informed, but I have to admit that I am not quite clear what Palamas thinks about his attribution to the energies or to the Person of the Holy Spirit. When he says, for example, "'The new spirit and the new heart' of

---

[9] O. Clément, *op. cit.* (footnote 7). p. 450. Amphilokios Radovic, *op. cit.* (footnote 1) shows that Palamas affirmed the procession of the Holy Spirit only from the Father, but that the Spirit also receives the divine essence from the Son (pp. 27ff.); he devotes pp. 42–43 to Gregory of Cyprus. In this context, it is also worth quoting Paul Evdokimov, *L'Esprit Saint dans la tradition orthodoxe* (Paris, 1969), p. 63: "The distinction between essence and energy is the first of the possible solutions of the *Filioque* in the light of the Eastern tradition. It postulates the distinction and identity of the Spirit (to *Pneuma* with the article) as hypostasis and of Spirit (*Pneuma* without the article) as energy. At the level of the common essence, the Spirit as hypostasis proceeds from the Father alone, although conjointly with the Son on whom he rests. As divine energy, Palamas teaches, 'the Spirit is poured out from the Father through the Son and, if one wants, from the Son' [quoted by J. Meyendorff, *Introduction, op. cit.*, p. 315 (*A Study, op. cit.*, p. 230)]. The solution, then, is to be found in the distinction between the hypostasis of the Holy Spirit and the energy that it manifests ex Patre Filioque."

Ezek 36:26 are created things, . . . whereas the Spirit of God given to the new heart (Ezek 27:5) is the Holy Spirit,"[10] is he speaking about the uncreated energies or the Person of the Holy Spirit? Again, when he says that the energies are nothing but the Holy Spirit, but that they are not the divine essence,[11] is he referring to the energies inhypostatized in the Holy Spirit or to the third Person of the Trinity? This may, of course, have to do with the fact that Palamas gives the name of Holy Spirit both to the uncreated energies and to the hypostasis. He says, for example:

> When you hear him (that is, Cyril of Alexandria) say that the Holy Spirit proceeds from the two, because he comes essentially from the Father through the Son, you should understand his teaching in this sense: it is the powers and essential energies of God which pour out, not the divine hypostasis of the Spirit.[12]

What the Fathers called *energeia* is the supernatural action of God, which is his Spirit—Father, Son and Spirit are the first subject, his power and his act.[13] Or else they spoke of the energies of the Spirit

---

[10] Quoted by J. Meyendorif, *A Study*, *op. cit.*, (footnote 1). p. 164.

[11] *Against Akindynos*, II, 17, quoted by J. Meyendorff, *A Study*, *op. cit.*, p. 225.

[12] *Apodictic Treatises*, quoted by J. Meyendorff, *A Study*, *op. cit.*, p. 230.

[13] See the many texts, together with full commentaries, in T. de Régnon, *Etudes de theólogie positive sur la Sainte Trinitè*, IV (Paris, 1898),

and meant by this his gifts, given to believers, but caused by him.[14]

This at once gives rise to the question—widely discussed by Palamas's opponents[15] of the continuity between the statements made by the Fathers and Palamas's systematic treatment of the subject. This whole question would be well worth examining in depth and with scholarly objectivity.[16] It would, in my opinion, certainly be possible to dispute the meaning of the texts of the Cappadocian Fathers and John Damascene that have been quoted in

---

pp. 425–465. This is, in particular, what is found in Athanasius, *Ad Ser.* I, 19, 20 and 31; III, 5. See also G. L. Prestige, *God in Patristic Thought*, 2nd ed. (London, 1952). pp. 257ff.

[14] This seems to me to be the case in the *Const. Apost.* V, 20, 4, with regard to Pentecost: "We have been filled with his energy and have spoken in new tongues," and in Maximus the Confessor, *Q. ad Thal.* 63 (*PG* 90, 672); *Theol. Polem.* 1 (*PG* 91, 33). In his anti-Monothelite struggle, Maximus spoke of divine energy in the sense of the active faculty of a nature or essence. For him, however, it was the creative causality and not the energies in the sense in which Palamas distinguished them from the essence and the hypostases; that, at least, is how J.-M. Garrigues interprets it; *op. cit.* (footnote 1).

[15] J. S. Nadal, *op. cit.* (footnote 1).

[16] All that we have at present is this partial study: E. von Ivanka, "Palamismus und Vätertradition," *L'Eglise et les Eglises. Mélanges Lambert Beauduin* (Chevetogne, 1954), II, pp. 29–46, who concluded that the texts in question do not speak of a real distinction in God himself, but of a distinction made by our spirit, which can only think in distinctions; see also J. P. Houdret, *op. cit.* (note 1). This conclusion is of crucial importance.

favour of Palamas's thesis.[17] The ante-Nicene Fathers, and in particular Athanasius, always denied that there could have been any procession in God other than that of the Persons. According to them, apart from the hypostases, only creatures proceeded from God. In opposition to Eunomius, according to whom the term *agennētos* adequately expressed the essence of God, the Fathers stressed the unknowable aspect of that essence. God, they believed, could only be known by his properties and works, and Basil of Caesarea called these his "energies," which, he claimed, "descend towards us, while his substance remains inaccessible."[18] The Fathers frequently expressed this distinction by using the terms *kat' auton* (God in himself) and *ta peri auton* or *peri autou* ("about him," in other words, what can be known and said about him, that is, on the basis of his properties and his activity) or *peri tēn phusin*.[19] André de Halleux, who is a considerable expert in this field, has, however, defended the interpretation of *peri auton*

---

[17] G. Florovsky, "Grégoire Palamas et la patristique," *Istina*, 8 (1961–1962). 113–125, especially 122 (only Basil of Caesarea, *Ep.* 234 *ad Amphilochium*, and John Damascene, *De fide orthod.* I, 14); G. Philips, *op, cit*, (footnote 22), 254.

[18] Basil of Caesarea, *Contra Eunom.* I, 4 (*PG* 29, 544); *Ep.* 234 *ed Amphilochium* 1 (*PG* 32, 869 A–B).

[19] See, for example, Gregory Nazianzen, *Orat.* 38, 7 (*PG* 36, 317B); 45, 3 (*PG* 36, 525C); Maximus the Confessor, *Centuries on Charity*, IV, 7 (*PG* 90, 1049A); *First Century on Theology and the Economy*, 48 (*PG* 90, 1100D); John Damascene, *De fide Orthod.* I, 4 and 10 (*PG* 94, 800C and 840).

which is favourable to Palamas.[20] From the philological point of view, he is clearly right, since *peri* followed by the accusative certainly means "around" or "in connection with." The question as to what theological or metaphysical conclusion should be drawn from the term, however, still remains. Did the Fathers postulate a kind of corona of divine energies which were active *ad extra*, which could be shared and which were ontologically and really distinct from the divine essence and the hypostases? E. von Ivanka, who is also a considerable expert, disputes this (see footnote 16). The problem has, in my opinion, not yet been fully cleared up, and I am in no position to decide. I am, however, impressed by the formal decision reached by so many Greek and Slav Orthodox theologians, who are in the best position to judge and interpret the writings of those who have borne witness to their own tradition.

We must now consider the question whether Palamism can be accepted by Western Catholicism or whether it is irreconcilably contrary to our teaching—and to our faith? The negative and critical position has been held, with varying shades of emphasis, by M.

---

[20] A. de Halleux, *op. cit.* (footnote 1), 484: "The contrast that the Cappadocian Fathers expressed by the words *kat' auton* and *peri auton* cannot be translated as that between God as he is in himself and what we are able to know about him. When it is followed by the accusative, the preposition *peri* usually means "around" and not "about" in this sense. By *peri auton* the Fathers therefore meant what is "around" or what surrounds the essence of God, the radiation of light coming from the dark nucleus of the essence.... This *peri auton* is not what God reveals of his *kat' auton*, that is, the essence as we are able to know it, the simple perceived as many. It is rather a flowing that is distinct in God himself from the inaccessible source of his being."

Jugie, S. Guichardan (see footnote 1), E. Candal,[21] and those who contributed to the 1974 number of *Istina* (see also footnote 1). On the other hand, there have been as many specialists in this sphere who have regarded it as possible to reconcile Palamism with the Catholic faith.[22] I say quite deliberately the "Catholic faith," because, if we are thinking of the theology of Augustine or Thomas Aquinas, we are bound to admit that, after reading Palamas openly

---

[21] Many publications are listed in D. Stiernon's bulletin on Palamism, *op. cit.* (footnote 1).

[22] I would mention here, in chronological order and for the most part in accordance with D. Stiernon's very valuable bulletin, *op. cit.*, to which the page numbers in brackets refer: G. Habra, "The Source of the Doctrine of Gregory Palamas on the Divine Energies," *ECQ*,12 (1957-1958). 244-252. 294-303, 338-347 (311); P. Bossuyt, "Hesychasmus en katholieke theologie, *Bijdragen* (1964), 229-238 (306); M. Strohm, "Die Lehre von der Einfachheit Gottes. Ein dogmatischer Streitpunkt zwischen Griechen und Lateiner," *Kyrios*, New Series, 7 (1967), 215-228; *idem*, "Die Lehre von der Energeia Gottes, " *ibid.*, 8 (1968), 63-84; 9 (1969), 31-41 (309-311); J. Kuhlmann, *Die Taten des einfachen Gottes. Eine römisch-katholische Stellungnahme zum Palamismus (Das östliche Christentum*, New Series, 21) (Würzburg, 1968) (294-299), with reference to a criticism by B. Schultze, *Or. Chr.* period, 36 (1970), 135-142; G. Philips, "La grâce chez les Orientaux," *ETL*, 48 (1972), 37-50, reprinted in *L'union personnelle avec le Dieu vivant. Essai sur l'origine et le* sens *de la grâce créée (Bibl. ETL*, XXXVI) (Gembloux, 1972). 241-260 (I shall be returning to this article by G. Philips, because his position has not received the attention that it deserves); A. de Halleux, "Palamisme et Scolastique," *RTL*, 4 (1973), 409-422; *idem*, "Orthodoxie et Catholicisme: du personnalisme en pneumatologie," *ibid.*, 6 (1975). 3-30: *idem*, "Palamisme et tradition," *op. cit.* (footnote 1). See also the following note.

and sympathetically and after recognizing very wide possibilities of agreement, there are still many great divergences. This ground has been covered to a great extent by Cardinal Journet on the basis of Jean Meyendorff's excellent book.[23] The distinction between faith and theology is quite fundamental—so much so that T. de Régnon referred to it again and again throughout the four volumes of his work on the Trinity.

Cardinal Journet has pointed out first of all that there is no opposition between Palamism and the Catholic faith with regard to the following articles: the natural and the supernatural order, Christ and the Eucharist, the Church as a mystical reality, the Virgin Mary and the saints. There are divergencies in the case of that very ambiguous term "original sin," the immaculate conception of Mary, and the procession of the Holy Spirit from the Father *and the Son* through the same spiration. The question of the real distinction between the essence and the divine energies, however, still remains, and this distinction is required by the affirmation of the full truth of our deification. The doctrine of the light of Mount Tabor is only an application of that distinction. I believe, together with Cardinal Journet, J.-M. Garrigues, G. Philips and, ultimately, also J. Kuhlmann (*op. cit.* (footnote 22), pp. 43–57), that this difference comes from the idea of participation. Let us look at this question more closely. Kuhlmann and Journet have both compared the same Pseudo-Dionysian texts as interpreted by Thomas Aquinas (and Maximus the Confessor) on the one hand and by

---

[23] C. Journet, "Palamisme et thomisme. A propos d'un livre récent," *RThom*, 60 (1960), 429–452.

Palamas on the other. To "participate" means to "take part," *partem capere*. Palamas interprets this as taking part in God entitatively and ontologically, but this participation cannot be in his essence, which cannot be communicated—it must be in the energies which emanate from that essence and which surround it. This, however, makes it possible for us to be deified in a literal and absolute sense—we become God and therefore we become, by grace, uncreated.[24] From the philosophical point of view, this Palamite idea of participation is clearly elementary and material,[25] one might almost say Neo-Platonic. The interpretation provided by Thomas Aquinas (and Maximus the Confessor), on the other hand, is Aristotelian, although it has taken from Plato a note of exemplarism. Maximus and Thomas comment on Pseudo-Dionysius' *Divine Names* in the following way: God, as a sovereign artist, lets his creatures participate, not in his divinity as such, which would be as impossible for us as it was for Palamas, but in the likenesses of his perfections of being—this is the exemplarism of the divine ideas—and through the efficient causality which confers existence. Thomas comments on *The Divine Names* II, 4 as follows:

---

[24] J. Meyendorff, *A Study, op. cit.* (footnote 1). pp. 176-177.

[25] Thus, according to Palamas, if man were to participate in God's essence, he would himself become omnipotent and there would consequently be an infinite number of divine hypostases: *Capita CL physica*, 108–109 (*PG* 150, 1193C-1196A). This accounts for G. Philips' comment, *op, cit.* (footnote 22). p. 253: "Palamas sees 'participation' as a division into almost materialized pieces, each participant possessing a fragment of the whole, which is clearly absurd. In his view, everything that can be shared can also be divided (*Cap*. 110; *PG* 150, 1196C; *Theoph*. 944 A)."

God is manifested by the effects that come from him. It is the Deity itself which to some extent proceeds in these effects, when it pours a likeness of itself into things according to their capacity, in such a way, however, that its excellence and its singularity remain intact in itself; these are not communicated to us and they remain hidden from our sight.[26]

This expresses the same sense of God's transcendence as I welcome and admire in the teaching of Gregory Palamas, but the concepts used by Thomas are, of course, quite different. The participation of which Thomas speaks is in a likeness of God's perfections and is realized in existence by the efficient causality of the absolute Being. There is no distinction in God himself between the divine essence that cannot be shared and the energies that are communicated, not even when it is a question of our supernatural participation. To the extent to which that participation includes created realities such as grace, charisms and gifts of the Holy Spirit,

---

[26] Thomas Aquinas, *In lib. de Divinis Nominibus expositio*, Turin ed., p. 46, No. 136. translated by Journet, *op. cit.* (footnote 23), p. 448. On p. 449, Journet has also translated Thomas' commentary on XI, 6 (*PG* 3, 956) (Thomas, *op. cit.* p. 346, no. 934), and that of Maximus, *Scholia in lib. de Div. Nom.* XI, 6 (*PG* 4, 401). J. Kuhlmann, *op. cit.* (footnote 22), pp. 43–57, has compared Thomas' and Palamas's commentaries on the *Divine Names*, XI, 6 (*PG* 3, 953ff.). For the idea of participation in the likeness, see also Thomas' fine passage *ST* IIIa, q. 23, a. 2 ad 3.

those realities have a status that is similar to that of natural realities. Participation, then, is not in perfections which are God's common perfections. It is rather in the divine nature as a principle of activities with God himself in view (see 2 Pet 1:3-4). The divine causality of grace produces in us principles of existence and action which enable us to attain the reality of God himself, that is, the Trinity, as the object of the life of the spirit, of knowledge and of love. These principles of action are limited (because they are created) in their entitative being, but they are effectively open to the infinite aspect of God himself, which they can attain without exhausting (*totum, non totaliter*). This is the effect of grace, of the theologal virtues and of the light of glory. And just as grace is that supernatural gift with which God himself is given, the indwelling in us of the divine Persons follows the gift of grace, with the enjoyment of their presence. This explanation, however, is as such not really dogmatic, but rather theological.

I do not dispute the underlying intention of Palamas's teaching, but find myself in disagreement with the concepts that he uses and his metaphysical mode of expression. Even if it is admitted that he is supported by several of the Fathers in his distinction *a parte rei* between the divine essence and the energies, he still only presents us with a theologoumenon in the precise sense in which this term has been defined by B. Bolotov:

> The opinions of the Fathers of the *one* and *undivided* Church are the opinions of those men among whom are found those who have rightly been called *hoi didaskaloi tēs*

oikoumenēs. . . . But, however widely accepted it may be, a *theologou-menon* does not constitute a dogma.[27]

Does Palamas's teaching constitute a dogma in the Orthodox Church? Certain Eastern Christians think so, including, for example, Professor Karminis and Archimandrite [now Bishop] Kallistos Ware [(now deceased)] (*op. cit.* (note 1 below), 58). Considerable importance has obviously also to be attached to the Council of Constantinople of 1351 and its decisions that were incorporated into the synodicon to be read on the First Sunday of Lent, the so-called Feast of Orthodoxy. (Are they still read then?) At the Council of Florence in 1439, the Greeks regarded the distinction between the divine energies and the uncreated character of the light of Mount Tabor as their teaching. Nowadays, Palamism is almost universally accepted by Orthodox theologians. But does all this evidence point to a dogma? There are strong reasons for doubting it.[28]

---

[27] B. Bolotov, "Thèses sur le 'Filioque'" (Fr. tr.), *Istina*, 17 (1972), 261–289, especially 262 and 263.

[28] For the "non-dogmatic" character in the strict sense of the distinction between essence and energies, despite the Council of 1351 and the Sunday anathemas of the Feast of Orthodoxy, see M. Jugie, *Theologia dogmatica*, *op. cit.* (footnote 1), pp. 132ff., who gives texts and summaries. What I. K. says, for example, in *Or. Chr. Period.*, 17 (1951), 488, is: "Is it a true dogma? Is it now still held as such in all the Eastern Churches? As for the Russian Church, it is well known that that Church ceased to affirm this from the eighteenth century onwards. In 1767, that Church radically changed the office of the Sunday of Orthodoxy and removed every trace of Palamism from it." See M. Jugie, *op. cit.*, pp. 176ff.

Did the Roman Catholic Church dogmatically condemn the Palamite theses at any time? J. Kuhlmann does not think so. He has examined the dogmatic statements concerning the vision of God.[29] Although the Latin participants at the Council of Florence regarded the Palamite thesis as heretical, no formal condemnation was pronounced by the Council itself. The Fathers of the Council spoke of *"intueri clare ipsum Deum trinum et unum sicuti est,"* but did not say *'per essentiam.'* Palamas might have agreed with that formula by seeing it as pointing to a vision of energies which are God. The Constitution *Benedictus Deus* of 1336 speaks of seeing *"essentiam divinam visione intuitiva et etiam faciali,"* and Kuhlmann's comment on this is that all that was intended was to oppose a vision of something created. Palamas may, however, have disputed the vision of the divine essence, but he certainly admitted participation in the divine nature (2 Pet 1:4), not *kata phusin*, but *kata charin*, that is, through grace. Kuhlmann has therefore concluded that, as far as Palamism is concerned, there is no obstacle to re-establishing communion with the East. Is he being too optimistic here? Mgr Gérard Philips, who was the king-pin in the Theological Commission of Vatican II, has come to the same conclusion. This is, in my opinion, a firm guarantee.

---

[29] J. Kuhlmann, *op. cit.* (footnote 22), pp. 108–125, for the Council of Florence (*DS* 1305); pp. 126–135 for the Constitution *Benedictus Deus* of Benedict XII, 29 January 1336 (*DS* 1000–1001).

Index

A
anti-Palamites, 3, 12
Aquinas, 4, 30, 66, 112, 120–23
Athos, monks of, 91, 97, 101
Augustine, 17, 29, 55, 120

B
Barlaam, 2, 21, 95–98, 110
Barlaamites, 95, 99–100
Basil, 22, 56, 94, 118
Blessed Virgin Mary, x, 35, 65, 68–86, 89–90, 121
Byzantine Catholics, 43
Byzantine Church, 9, 44–45, 73, 80, 91–92

C
Calecas, Manuel, 67
Canonization of Palamas, 101
Cappadocian Fathers, 117, 119
Cardinal Henri, 41
Cardinal Journet, 121
Catherine Mowry LaCugna, 66
Catholic Archbishop of Corfu, 76
Catholic Faith, 6, 31, 90, 120–21
Catholics, 7–8, 10–12, 25–26, 31, 34, 47, 49, 54–55, 57, 64, 66, 68, 101–2
Catholics United for the Faith (CUF), 129
Catholic theologians, 6, 9, 15, 52, 75–76, 89, 109
Christ, 5, 7, 18, 20–23, 33–35, 39–41, 64–65, 68–69, 72, 74, 76-77, 79–80, 82, 84, 90, 109
Christian Church, 13–14, 23, 25–26, 35, 62, 66, 101, 104–5
Christology, 65, 103, 105

Clément, 108, 113–15
Communion of Saints, 105
Congar, Yves, 6, 107
Coniaris, Anthony M., 61-64, 89
Constantinople, 3, 45, 48, 95, 97–98, 100, 110, 114, 125

D
Damascene, John, 117–18
deification, 17, 22–24, 26–28, 47, 66, 103–5, 111, 115, 121
denial, 28, 34–35, 55, 57–58, 103
divine essence, 1, 7–8, 15–16, 18, 22, 24, 28–29, 50, 52, 54, 66–67, 92, 102, 111–13, 115–16, 123–24
divine grace, 2–3, 5–16, 18–19, 24–31, 36–39, 41, 44, 48–53, 55, 58, 61–64, 66–67, 72–76, 78–79, 81–82, 84–85, 88–90, 104–5, 110–13, 122–26
divine nature, 12–13, 19, 23–25, 29, 47, 51, 53, 63, 67, 104, 124, 126
Divine Persons, 16–17, 30, 46, 51, 67, 71, 113, 124
divinization, 2, 5, 11, 13, 16–17, 23–26, 28–31, 50, 63, 66–67, 76
dogma, 3, 9, 36–38, 47, 57, 64–65, 67–68, 73, 79, 101, 125
Dvornik, Francis, 73

E
Eastern Churches, 10–11, 23–24, 43, 56, 75, 82, 108, 125
Eastern Fathers, 23–24, 94
Eastern Orthodox, 3, 25, 36–37, 64, 89, 129
ecumenical council, 15, 27, 36–38, 51, 59, 68
energies, uncreated divine, viii–ix, 2–6, 8–9, 12–17, 22–23, 27-28, 32, 40, 43–49, 50–55, 57, 59, 62–64, 66–67, 72–73, 75–80, 89, 93–95, 104–5, 108, 110–18, 116, 121–26
essence, viii–x, 2–4, 8–10, 12–16, 27–28, 44–47, 50–53, 55, 63–64, 66–67, 92–94, 111–13, 117–19, 121–22
essence and energy, ix, 32, 57, 63, 94, 115

Index 129

F
faith, 3, 19–21, 36, 49–50, 61, 89, 119, 121
Filioque, 8, 10, 19, 32, 37, 47, 54, 95, 108, 114–15, 125

G
glory, 17–21, 26, 49–50, 62, 82–83, 85, 87, 89, 112, 124
Gregory Palamas's teaching, ix, xi, 1–2, 6–7, 13–15, 17, 25, 33, 35, 43–45, 50–51, 61, 63–69, 71–89, 98–101, 107–26

H
Hesychasm, 2, 11, 33, 48, 59, 91–102, 109
Hesychastic Controversy, 3, 6, 59
Hesychasts, 4, 14, 64, 91–96, 98–99, 101, 112
holiness, 78–80, 90, 105
Holy Spirit, 6, 11, 17, 23–24, 28, 29-30, 32–34, 51, 53–54, 57, 74, 105, 108, 111, 113–17, 121, 123
Holy Trinity, 16, 19, 23, 49–51, 53, 55, 108, 113
homilies, 25, 34–35, 43, 68–75, 77, 80, 83–90, 107
human nature, 18, 80, 104–5
hypostases, 17, 29, 111–19

I
Immaculate Conception, 7, 38, 72–79, 90, 121

J
Jugie, Martin, 73

L
Light, uncreated, 13, 16–17, 20, 38, 46, 48, 58, 63, 92–94, 97, 100
Lumen Gentium, 36, 105

M
Mariology, 65–89
Maximus, 56, 105, 117–18, 121–23
Meyendorff, 37, 40, 69, 71–72, 107–8, 110, 112–13, 115–16,

122
Mohila, Peter, 19–20, 50
monks, 1, 4, 7, 12, 48, 63, 91–93, 95–100, 109–10
Mount Tabor, 14–15, 46, 62–63, 110, 112, 121, 125

N
nature, 26–27, 30, 32, 46–47, 50, 75, 80, 84, 86, 89–90, 114, 117
neo-Palamites, 9, 15, 22, 27, 29–30, 36, 51, 55, 57
neo-Palamite school of theology, 1, 9, 45
Nichols, Aidan, 15, 52

O
Orthodox Church, x, 12, 44, 47, 57, 61–62, 65, 89, 91, 99–102, 125
Orthodoxy, 2, 4, 43, 56–57, 95, 98, 100, 125

P
Palamas, viii–x, 1–6, 9–10, 12–13, 15–17, 20–21, 27–30, 32–37, 44–49, 51–57, 61–64, 66–80, 82–90, 95–100, 107–20, 122, 126
Palamism, 1–59, 66–67, 107–10, 113, 119–21, 125–26
Palamite error, 19
Palamites, 1, 3, 12, 20, 22, 49–50, 53, 56, 58, 108, 111–12
pantheism, 25, 30, 93
Particular Judgment, 54–55
patriarch, 33, 58, 98–100
Peter, 25, 34–37, 39–40, 58–59
Pope Benedict XII, 29, 55

R
Roman Catholic, 40, 126

S
sanctification, 16–17, 26, 28, 50
Son, 24, 32, 34–35, 51, 54, 57, 69, 81, 86, 104, 109, 111, 113–16
Spiteris, Yannis, 76

St. Andrew, 21
St. Anne, 79
St. Athanasius, 30
St. Augustine, 29, 55
St. Bernard, 102
St. Irenaeus, 24
St. Joachim, 79
St. John, 5, 18, 20, 49
St. John Damascene, 21
St. John Paul II, 10-11, 24
  Pope, 10, 23, 43
St. Louis, 27
St. Luke, 85
St. Paul, 18
St. Thomas Aquinas, 30, 47, 50, 52, 80, 94, 96, 122-23
Supra-Essence, 27, 51–52

T
theosis, 5–6, 11, 13, 23–25, 48, 62–63
Thomism, 3
Thomists, 88, 111
Transfiguration, 2, 13, 15, 20–22, 26, 38, 48, 62–63, 92, 98, 102, 107

V
Vicar of Christ, 58

About the Author

A convert from Greek Orthodoxy, James Likoudis is an internationally known apologist, who has dedicated his life to reconciling his Eastern Orthodox brethren with the Catholic Church. He excels in analyzing the key issues that separate Catholics and Orthodox, including regarding papal and conciliar history, and he cherishes all we hold in common in Christ.

Likoudis served for more than twenty-five years at the lay apostolate Catholics United for the Faith (CUF), including as president. He is the author of many books including *The Pope, The Council, and The Mass*; *The Divine Primacy of the Bishop of Rome and Modern Eastern Orthodoxy*; and *Heralds of a Catholic Russia*. He has written and lectured widely on ecumenism, religious education, liturgy, sex education, family life, and the role of the laity in the Church. He is also a former college instructor in history and government, with over twenty years of teaching experience. Likoudis received an honorary Doctorate of Divinity from Sacred Heart Major Seminary in Detroit in 2020. He and his late wife Ruth have six children, thirty-five grandchildren, and forty-five great-grandchildren.

Dear reader,

We are excited to introduce to you the Likoudis Legacy Foundation—a Catholic theological and evangelistic initiative aimed at preserving and perpetuating the profound impact of James Likoudis, an eminent American, Catholic theologian, and author.

We seek to accomplish this by highlighting his contributions to the Holy Catholic Church in the fields of Ecumenism, Liturgy, Family Life, Sex Education, Theology of the Laity, Mariology, Apologetics, Morality, and Doctrine. We plan to use these works as inspiration for understanding and sharing the Catholic Faith.

Likoudis's lifelong dedication to Christian Unity—particularly with the Eastern Orthodox—and defending Catholic orthodoxy, rooted in tradition and in the ideals of the Second Vatican Council, has left an indelible mark on today's Catholic landscape.

The Foundation's vision extends beyond merely acknowledging Likoudis's past achievements, however. It seeks to honor James Likoudis by inspiring future generations to continue his work, through fostering a deep understanding of it by way of continued research and application to contemporary Church and Society.

For more information about this initiative, please visit us online at http://www.likoudislegacy.com.

www.ingramcontent.com/pod-product-compliance
Lightning Source LLC
LaVergne TN
LVHW020932090426
835512LV00020B/3317